CATHOLICISM USA

**A Portrait of the Catholic Church
in the United States**

The Catholic Church Today

A three volume profile and reflection on the contemporary reality of the Catholic Church in the United States and around the world.

Bryan T. Froehle, Series Director
Mary L. Gautier, Series Editor

Center for Applied Research in the Apostolate
Georgetown University

I: CATHOLICISM USA
A Portrait of the Catholic Church in the United States

II: CATHOLICISM TODAY
A Global Portrait of a World Church

III: CHALLENGES AND OPPORTUNITIES
Catholicism in the Twenty-First Century

CATHOLICISM USA

**A Portrait of the Catholic Church
in the United States**

*Center for Applied Research in the Apostolate
Georgetown University*

**Bryan T. Froehle
Mary L. Gautier**

ORBIS BOOKS

Maryknoll, New York 10545

The Catholic Foreign Mission Society of America (Maryknoll) recruits and trains people for overseas missionary service. Through Orbis Books, Maryknoll aims to foster the international dialogue that is essential to mission. The books published, however, reflect the opinions of their authors and are not meant to represent the official position of the society.

To obtain more information about Maryknoll and Orbis Books, please visit our website at www.maryknoll.org.

Library of Congress Cataloging-in-Publication Data

Froehle, Bryan.
    The Catholic Church today / Bryan T. Froehle, Mary L. Gautier.
        p. cm.
    Includes bibliographical references and index.
    Contents: v. 1. Catholicism USA.
    ISBN 1-57075-272-9 (v. 1 : pbk.)
    1. Catholic Church – United States – Statistics. 2. United States – Church history – 20th century – Statistics. I. Gautier, Mary, 1952- II. Center for Applied Research in the Apostolate (U.S.) III. Title.

BX 1406.2 .F74 2000
282'.73'09051–dc21   00-037483

The forms of the apostolate should be properly adapted to current needs not only in terms of spiritual and moral conditions, but also of social, demographic, and economic ones. Religious and social surveys, made through offices of pastoral sociology, contribute greatly to the effective and fruitful attainment of that goal, and they are cordially recommended.

—*Christus Dominus*, n.17
(Decree of the Second Vatican Council on the Pastoral Office of Bishops in the Church, October 28, 1965)

Contents

PART I
CHANGES AND CONTINUITIES
AMONG U.S. CATHOLICS

List of Tables, Figures, and Maps

statistical sources are varied and broad, including official or quasi-official publications such as the *Annuarium Statisticum Ecclesiae* and the *Annuario Pontificio*, both published by the Vatican, and *The Official Catholic Directory*, published by Reed Elsevier, Incorporated. We are particularly indebted to our collaboration with Jeanne Hanline, editor of *The Official Catholic Directory*, who first worked under P.J. Kenedy before he sold the rights to the *Directory* name in the late 1970s. Her experience and collaborative spirit make her an unsung hero in Catholic research.

Other sources include many of CARA's own original data-gathering projects, such as the *Catholic Ministry Formation Directory*, an annual report and directory for U.S. institutions that prepare candidates for priesthood, the diaconate, and lay ministry; the *National Parish Inventory*, a CARA database on every parish in the United States; and the *Directory of Religious Institutes*, on existing and emerging religious institutes in the United States. Other data come from specific research we or our colleagues have conducted over the past few decades.

All databases have been either designed or reviewed by CARA and members of our project team that includes Todd Pfeiffer and Prakit Hirankarn, who wrote the code and designed the databases compiled and refined for this project. Prakit, along with Sandra Lara, Silvia Lara, and others, diligently and professionally entered much of the data from published sources.

Finally, we would be remiss if we did not acknowledge the leadership, encouragement, and vision of Bishop William B. Friend, the current Chair of CARA's Board of Directors, along with all other members of CARA's Board and its Research Advisors.

Bryan T. Froehle and Mary L. Gautier
Center for Applied Research in the Apostolate
Georgetown University
March 2000

PART I

Changes and Continuities among U.S. Catholics

In 1900, about one in seven people in the U.S. was Catholic, almost 11 million in a population of 76 million. With several notable exceptions, most were working-class European immigrants or the children of immigrants who lived in the large urban centers of the Northeast and Midwest.

One hundred years later, almost one in four people in the U.S. is Catholic, some 60 million in a population of 267 million. Many of the descendants of those turn of the century Catholics are now highly educated professionals who live in places far different from the dense urban immigrant communities that nurtured their forebears. At the same time, a substantial minority of U.S. Catholics today are immigrants – now primarily from Latin America and, to a lesser extent, from Asia and Africa. As the Catholic community in the U.S. has grown in size and complexity, it has also come to reflect more and more closely the regional, social, and ethnic diversity of the United States.

The first part of this portrait of Catholicism in the United States examines broad social and demographic shifts among Catholics in the United States over the twentieth century. Not surprisingly, as Catholics grew in number and diversity, their beliefs and practices experienced both changes and continuities.

Chapter 1 focuses on demographic changes over the twentieth century, including changes in the Catholic population and its socio-economic status.

It also presents comparative population figures and growth rates for the Catholic population of the United States.

Chapter 2 looks at patterns in Catholic values and attitudes over the twentieth century. Much is based on research over recent decades, although an effort has been made to present a relevant historical context. As this chapter suggests, Catholics in the United States continue to have a cultural and attitudinal distinctiveness that sets them apart as a group in spite of the disappearance of some of the structural and institutional boundaries of the pre-Vatican II Church and the Catholic communities of the first half of the century.

A general portrait of contemporary Catholicism can only provide a brief sketch of topics for which a considerable array of books and articles already exist. Where possible, therefore, the endnotes and bibliography name a few selected sources that offer more detail.

CHAPTER 1

The Catholic Population

CHANGES OVER THE TWENTIETH CENTURY

Catholicism is the most common religious identity in the United States. Recent national surveys report that about 27 percent of the U.S. population identifies as Catholic. According to parish-based and diocesan-reported data given in Table 1.1, Catholics grew from 14 percent to 22 percent of the U.S. population during the course of the twentieth century.[1] Catholics made up 38.9 percent of the total of adherents to the 500 largest Judeo-Christian religious bodies surveyed in a 1990 study of religious life and membership in the United States.[2]

According to diocesan-reported figures, shown here in Table 1.1, Catholic population initially grew by about 166 percent in the period

Table 1.1. Catholic Presence in the United States: Increases over the Twentieth Century

Year	Catholics	U.S. Population	Percent Catholic
1900	10,774,989	76,094,000	14%
1950	28,634,878	152,271,417	19%
1998*	59,156,237	267,636,061	22%

*At the time of writing, this was the most recent year for which figures were available. This year is used in many of the tables that follow for that reason.

between 1900 and 1950. Since 1950, Catholic population has again more than doubled, increasing by 106 percent between 1950 and 1998. Although immigration is in many ways a significant, defining phenomenon in the history of U.S. Catholics, the twentieth-century rise in population has had more to do with natural increase than with immigration. The U.S. population as a whole increased by more than 75 percent during the second half of the century, as the post-World War II generation nicknamed the "Baby Boomers" (birth years 1943 to 1960) entered the picture. Catholic households, not surprisingly, grew very quickly. Catholics were younger than the population as a whole and had settled in regions where immediate postwar prosperity was most pronounced.

Comparisons to Other Countries
The United States has the fourth largest Catholic population of any country in the world.[3] Over the past 30 years, the Catholic population in the U.S. has also come to surpass the Catholic population of any other developed country. As Table 1.2 shows, the only large European country with a Catholic population growth rate close to that of the United States is Poland.

Table 1.2. Catholic Population of Countries with 30 Million or More Catholics in 1997				
			Growth	
	1997	**1970**	**Numeric**	**Percent**
Brazil	134,818,000	81,815,000	53,003,000	65%
Mexico	86,305,000	46,007,000	40,298,000	88
Philippines	58,735,000	31,025,000	27,710,000	89
United States	57,047,000	45,920,000	11,127,000	24
Italy	55,599,000	52,500,000	3,099,000	6
France	47,773,000	45,698,000	2,075,000	5
Spain	36,956,000	33,203,000	3,753,000	11
Poland	36,853,000	30,601,000	6,252,000	20
Colombia	32,260,000	20,505,000	11,755,000	57
Argentina	31,546,000	21,191,000	10,355,000	49

Comparisons to Other Religious Bodies
Though the United States is still predominantly a Protestant country – about 60 percent of the population identifies as Protestant on recent surveys – Catholics number more than the combined membership figures of the next ten largest religious bodies.[4]

Table 1.3. Current Membership Figures for Religious Bodies in the United States with More Than One Million Members

	Current	**1970**	**Change**	**Percent**
Catholic Church	59,156,237	47,872,089	+11,284,148	+24%
Southern Baptist Convention	15,891,514	11,628,032	+4,263,482	+37%
United Methodist Church	8,496,047	10,671,774	-2,175,727	-20%
National Baptist Convention, USA	8,200,000	5,500,000	+2,700,000	+49%
Church of God in Christ	5,499,875	425,000	+5,074,875	+1194%
Evangelical Lutheran Church in America*	5,178,225	5,650,304	- 472,079	-8%
Church of Jesus Christ of Latter-Day Saints	4,923,100	2,073,146	+2,849,954	+137%
Presbyterian Church USA*	2,587,674	4,049,391	-1,461,717	-36%
National Baptist Convention of America, Inc.	3,500,000	2,688,799	+ 811,201	+30%
African Methodist Episcopal Church	3,500,000	1,950,000	+1,550,000	+79%
Episcopal Church	2,536,550	3,285,826	-749,276	-23%
Lutheran Church- Missouri Synod	2,603,036	2,788,536	-185,500	-7%
Progressive National Baptist Convention	2,500,000	521,692	+1,978,308	+379%
National Missionary Baptist Convention of America	2,500,000	—	+2,500,000	—
Assemblies of God	2,494,574	625,027	+1,869,547	+299%
Orthodox Church in America	2,000,000	1,000,000	+1,000,000	+100%
Greek Orthodox Diocese of America	1,954,500	1,950,000	+4,500	0%
Churches of Christ	1,800,000	2,400,000	-600,000	-25%
United Church of Christ	1,438,181	1,960,608	-522,427	-27%
African Episcopal Zion Church	1,252,369	940,000	+312,397	+33%
Bible Baptist Fellowship	1,200,000	—	+1,200,000	—
Christian Churches and Churches of Christ	1,071,616	1,020,751	+50,865	+5%
Pentecostal Assemblies of the World, Inc.	1,000,000	45,000	+955,000	+2122%

*Since this body was formed by a merger after 1970, the membership figures for 1970 include those of its predecessor organizations.

African Americans converted as they moved to Catholic neighborhoods and sent their children to Catholic schools, perhaps inspired by the pioneering efforts of African American Catholic leaders, such as Bishop James Augustine Healy and other black clergy, and Mother Mary Elizabeth Lange along with the order she founded, the Oblate Sisters of Providence. Immigration from Africa, the Caribbean, and Latin America has also augmented the African American Catholic population.[6]

Table 1.4. Shifts in Catholic Population by Census Region			
Catholic percent of U.S. population in each region given in parentheses			
	1998	**1950**	**Change**
Northeast	19,897,450	13,092,996	+52%
	(38%)	(33%)	
Midwest	14,225,372	8,963,156	+59%
	(23%)	(20%)	
South	11,231,745	3,796,300	+196%
	(12%)	(8%)	
West	13,354,145	3,695,266	+261%
	(22%)	(18%)	
Total	58,708,712	29,547,718	+99%
	(22%)	(20%)	

These diverse migrations, both from other countries and from within the U.S., have resulted in increases in Catholic population in every region. As Table 1.4 shows, these shifts have been fairly sizeable over the past half century.[7]

Catholics are perhaps most similar to Methodists in their geographic dispersion. Like Methodists, Catholics are also relatively widely dispersed throughout the country.[8] However, the two have had opposite demographic trajectories: Methodists were principally based first in small towns in the interior of the U.S. and then spread to the cities. The Catholic population, on the other hand, grew from successful efforts to maintain the religious allegiance of residents and immigrants of different ethnic origin and social class during the late nineteenth and early twentieth centuries. Catholic immigrants tended to cluster together in ethnic enclaves, principally in cities, but also in smaller towns and rural areas. As a result, Catholicism remains relatively more concentrated in metropolitan areas and relatively more ethnically and economically diverse compared to specific Protestant denominations.

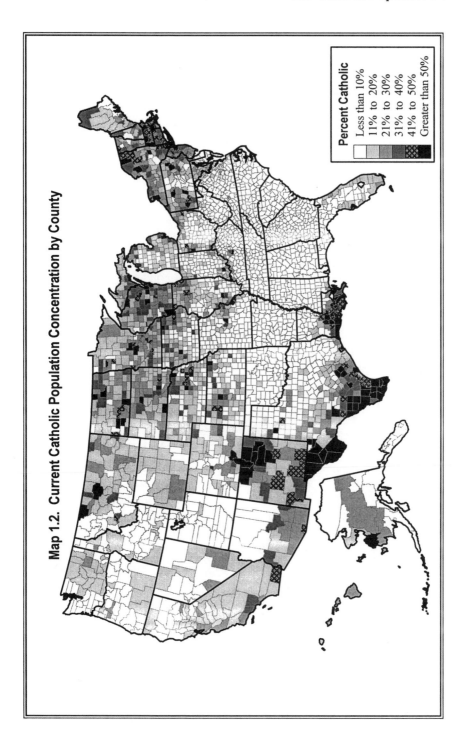

Map 1.2. Current Catholic Population Concentration by County

Percent Catholic

Less than 10%
11% to 20%
21% to 30%
31% to 40%
41% to 50%
Greater than 50%

Table 1.5. Counties and Catholic Population

Catholic Concentration within Counties	Counties Number	Percent
10 percent or less Catholic	1,825	58%
More than 10 percent Catholic	1,316	42
Of these 1,316, counties that are:		
At least 20 percent Catholic	719	23
At least 30 percent Catholic	389	12
At least 40 percent Catholic	212	7
50 percent or more Catholic	127	4

As Table 1.5 shows, over 120 counties, just four percent of all counties in the U.S., are majority Catholic. In all, close to 400 counties have populations that are at least 30 percent Catholic. However, while these 400 counties are only 12 percent of all U.S. counties, their population is disproportionately large, representing include about 30 percent of the U.S. population.

Nearly 95 percent of all Catholics in the United States live in 42 percent of the counties, as does 70 percent of the U.S. population as a whole. Map 1.2 shows the dispersion of the Catholic population by counties.

CAUSES OF CATHOLIC POPULATION GROWTH

The Impact of Immigration

Immigration caused most of the increase in Catholic population in the United States until open European immigration was replaced by strict quotas of the National Origins Act of 1924, passed during a time of considerable anti-immigrant and anti-Catholic sentiment. Table 1.6 shows the numbers of immigrants from each country in the century before 1924, the greatest period of European immigration to the United States.[9] Although no data exist for how many immigrants from this time identified with particular religious faiths, significant numbers came from predominantly Catholic countries or portions of European empires.

After 1924, the Catholic birth rate became the driving factor in Catholic population increase. Immigrant women tended to be in their child-bearing years, and this led to rapid increases in the Catholic population, since many children were born to Catholic immigrants soon after their arrival. Furthermore, having just recently left rural life, with its village culture and relatively large families, immigrant Catholics and their children in the big cities tended to have larger families and stronger bonds of mutual support than their Protestant contemporaries. Post-World War II prosperity during the late 1940s and 1950s also added to the ability of Catholics in the United States to have larger families. For its part, the Church in the United States carefully built structures to support and nurture these families.

Table 1.6. U.S. Immigration from 1824 to 1924: Top Ten Places of Origin		
Country	**Immigrants**	**Peak Year**
Germany	6,028,377	1882
Italy	4,719,825	1907
Ireland	4,592,595	1851
Great Britain	4,264,728	1888
Austria-Hungary	4,144,366	1907
Russia	3,343,480	1913
Canada	3,037,561	1924
Sweden	1,218,229	1882
Norway	805,367	1882
France	605,430	1824

Thus, for a variety of reasons, family size at mid-century was larger for Catholics than for Protestants. By the the mid-1980s, however, this had changed. If anything, the number of children born to non-Hispanic/Latino Catholic women today is somewhat lower than the national average.[10]

In recent times, significant Catholic population growth has again been fueled by immigration. The number of immigrants in the U.S. population as a whole has almost doubled over the past three decades since restrictions on non-European immigration were reduced after 1964.[11] During a recent five-year period, as Table 1.7 shows, a majority of immigrants to the United States came from Latin America and a significant minority from Asia.

Unlike earlier periods, relatively few immigrants are European. But similar to that earlier time, today's immigrants tend to come from countries with a relatively large Catholic population. However, this fact has less of an impact on Catholic population than it once did. Because the Catholic population is so much larger today it takes many more immigrants than it did once to change the composition of the Catholic population. In addition,

Table 1.7. Recent Sources of Legal Immigrants, 1991-1996

	Number	Percent
Total	**6,146,300**	**100%**
North America	**2,740,000**	**45**
Mexico	1,651,400	27
Caribbean	655,400	11
Central America	**342,800**	**6**
El Salvador	147,600	2
Guatemala	70,300	1
South America	**344,000**	**6**
Colombia	81,700	1
Peru	66,700	1
Asia	**1,941,800**	**32**
Philippines	348,500	6
Vietnam	317,900	5
Africa	**331,000**	**5**
Nigeria	37,900	>1
Ghana	18,000	>1
Europe	**875,600**	**14**
Former Soviet Union	339,900	6
Poland	130,200	2

From the *Statistical Abstracts of the United States: 1998*, Table No. 8, "Immigrants by Country of Birth, 1991 to 1996," shown by continent and by the two numerically largest contributing countries or subregions. Percentages may add up to more than 100 due to rounding.

immigrants from "Catholic" countries are less likely to be Catholic than before. Protestant missionaries have had enormous success over the past 50 years in Latin America, the Philippines, and other countries once considered almost entirely Catholic. Indeed, evidence exists that those who emigrate from these countries are somewhat less likely to be Catholic than those who stay behind.[12]   Also, Catholic identity has not been as successfully maintained among recent immigrants as in earlier times when a strong Catholic subculture and religious discrimination created boundaries that promoted Catholic identity. As a result, care should be taken not to extrapolate that contemporary immigrants from nominally Catholic regions, such as Latin America, are Catholics or will remain

Catholics, just as it was once assumed that all immigrants from principally Catholic regions of Europe, such as Italy, were Catholic.[13]

Intermarriage and Conversion

For most of the twentieth century, Catholics were largely resistant to religious intermarriage, for religious as well as cultural reasons – even intermarriage between members of different groups of ethnic Catholics was seen by some families as unacceptable. However, conversions to Catholicism often resulted from those religiously mixed marriages that did occur.

Religious intermarriage is much more common among Catholics today, and remains the single largest factor underlying the majority of adult conversions. This should not be surprising, given that a little over one-third of all marriages witnessed or registered by the Church are of a Catholic to a non-Catholic.

However, conversion of the non-Catholic spouse is no longer as strongly insisted upon or expected. Thus, in spite of an increasing number of interfaith marriages and increasing numbers of Catholics, adult conversions to Catholicism actually have declined since 1960.

At the same time, the number of Catholic baptisms of infants reported in the United States has held steady as a percentage of all U.S. births over the past 20 years, suggesting that the children produced by interfaith unions are still somewhat more likely to be raised Catholic – or at least baptized Catholic. The number of infant baptisms as a percentage of all U.S. births is not especially different from that of 1950, as Table 1.8 shows.[14] The relatively modest decline may be accounted for in part by reductions in the number of children born to Catholics relative to non-Catholics.

Table 1.8. Growth in the Catholic Population: Catholic Adult Conversions and Infant Baptisms			
Year	Adult Conversions	Infant Baptisms	Infant Baptisms to U.S. births
1950	121,950	1,095,494	27%
1960	131,641	1,486,193	31
1970	84,534	1,172,997	29
1980	88,942	1,032,574	26
1990	81,910	1,095,898	24
1998	82,110	970,247	25

achievement is also related to the broader orientation toward achievement present in immigrant culture; these patterns hold true for many Catholics, regardless of the type of school they attended.[17]

Table 1.10. Education Level of Catholics by Generation					
	All	**World War II**	**Silent**	**Vatican II**	**Young Adult**
High School or Less	26%	52%	41%	22%	21%
Some College	29	25	25	29	31
College Graduate	32	15	21	33	37
Graduate or Professional School	13	8	13	16	11

By the mid-1960s, the legacy of earlier European immigrations began to smooth out, and Catholics came to rank above Protestants on most Gallup poll indices of socioeconomic status. Within a decade, the average annual family income of white Catholics matched or exceeded white Protestant groups. Today, Catholics tend to be somewhat over-represented in upper- and middle-income groups.

Table 1.11. Household Income of Catholics by Generation					
	All	**World War II**	**Silent**	**Vatican II**	**Young Adult**
Less than $20,000	13%	42%	23%	7%	12%
$20,000-39,999	24	35	30	19	27
$40,000-59,999	25	11	22	26	25
$60,000-79,999	17	5	9	21	17
$80,000-99,999	9	4	5	11	9
$100,000 or more	12	3	11	16	10

Racial and Ethnic Diversity

The percentage of Catholics who belong to specific racial and ethnic minority groups roughly approaches that of the U.S. Census. The United States as a whole is approximately 83 percent white, 13 percent African American, 11 percent Hispanic, four percent Asian, and one percent Native American. Catholics today are about 78 percent white, with three percent African American, 16 percent Hispanic/Latino, two percent Asian, and one percent Native American. Some studies suggest that the proportion of

Catholics in the United States who are of Hispanic/Latino descent may be 18 percent, or perhaps even higher.[18]   Figure 1.1 shows data from the CARA Catholic Poll 2000 on the racial and ethnic distribution of Catholics.

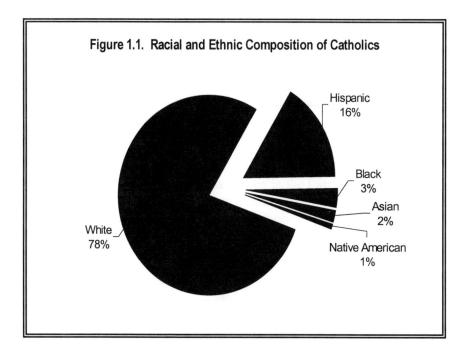

Figure 1.1. Racial and Ethnic Composition of Catholics

Hispanic 16%

Black 3%

Asian 2%

Native American 1%

White 78%

An important and often misunderstood aspect of racial and ethnic diversity among Catholics is the proportion of members of particular groups who are Catholic. This is especially the case for Hispanics/Latinos. While there are considerable data that show that the number and proportion of Hispanics/Latinos in both the general population and the Catholic population in the U.S. are increasing, it is important to note that the proportion of Hispanics/Latinos who identify as Catholics is decreasing. Figure 1.2 illustrates this trend, which is confirmed by data from the CARA Catholic Poll 2000. According to this most recent survey, 56 percent of Hispanics/Latinos in the United States today consider their religious background to be Catholic. One of the most reliable sources suggests that just over half of those from this background consider themselves Catholic. At the same time, the proportion of all Catholics who are Hispanic is increasing, as the second line in Figure 1.2 demonstrates. Thus, the Hispanic presence in the Catholic Church in the United States will continue to have an increasing presence among U.S. Catholics, but growth will not

CHAPTER 2

Behavior and Values of Catholics

At precisely the time of their ascent into the middle class and assimilation into the mainstream of U.S. society, Catholics experienced dramatic changes within Church life in the wake of the changes initiated by the Second Vatican Council. During these transition years, many Catholics came to a greater sense of openness regarding their faith and theological pluralism. Compared to their predecessors in the decades immediately before the Council, Catholics today are less obedient to some of the teachings of the Church, less united on certain tenets of their faith, and less observant in some of their religious practices.[1]

Today, active Catholics are more likely to disagree over specific moral teachings, Church authority, and the mission of the Church in public life. However, given the scope of changes, there is surprisingly little disagreement among Catholics over the core of their faith and what it means to be Catholic.[2]

Large majorities of Catholics today say that their Catholic faith is important to them and that they are satisfied with the Church and its leadership. CARA's Catholic Poll 2000, a telephone survey of over 2,500 randomly selected Catholics, finds that 85 percent of self-identified Catholics report that their Catholic faith is "somewhat" or "very" important to them and about three-fourths say they are "somewhat" or "very" satisfied with the way the Church meets their spiritual needs (77 percent) and with the leadership of the Church (74 percent).

Table 2.1, above, presents findings from the CARA Catholic Poll 2000, which show that 34 percent of all Catholics report attending Mass at least once every week. Another 26 percent report attending on a regular basis, either "once or twice a month" or "almost every week." Older Catholics are more likely than younger Catholics to be frequent Mass attenders.

Catholic Marriage

Prior to Vatican II, the Church generally discouraged Catholics from marrying those of other faiths, primarily because of concerns that children produced by such a union would not be raised in the faith. Nevertheless, approximately 25 percent of all sacramental marriages in the U.S. were between Catholics and non-Catholics at that time. These marriages were witnessed by a priest but did not take place as part of a wedding Mass. Weddings conducted during non-Catholic religious services or civil marriages performed by a justice of the peace or other officials were much less common among Catholics.

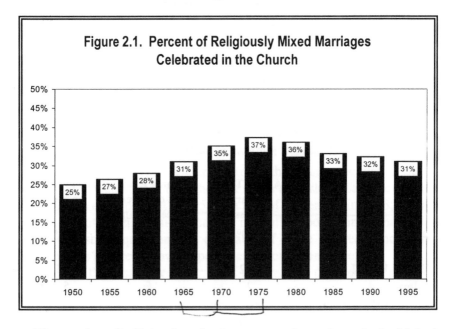

Figure 2.1. Percent of Religiously Mixed Marriages Celebrated in the Church

The number of religiously mixed sacramental marriages in the United States peaked in 1975, at about 37 percent of all sacramental marriages, as shown in Figure 2.1. Since then, the proportion of interfaith marriages has been dropping. But the number of sacramental marriages as a proportion of all marriages has also been decreasing. In 1970, 20 percent of all U.S. marriages were witnessed by a Catholic priest. Ten years later, that number had declined to 15 percent, and by 1990 it was 13 percent. The divergence

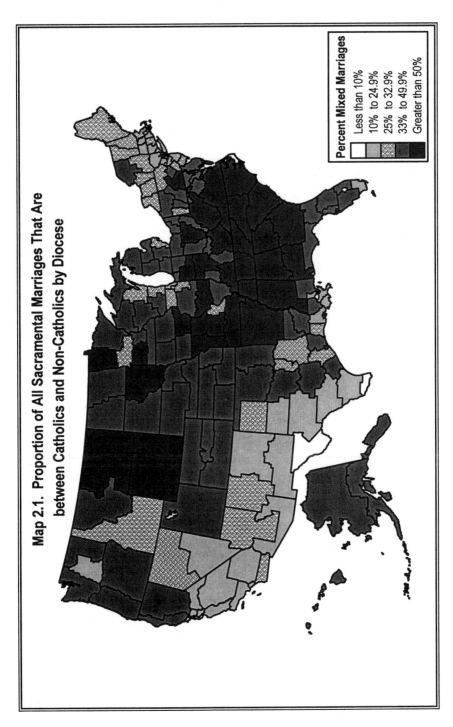

Map 2.1. Proportion of All Sacramental Marriages That Are between Catholics and Non-Catholics by Diocese

Percent Mixed Marriages

Less than 10%
10% to 24.9%
25% to 32.9%
33% to 49.9%
Greater than 50%

Table 2.3. Important Aspects of Being Catholic
Percent of Catholics who identify each as being important

	Percent
Helping those in need	97%
Passing on the faith to the next generation	91
Eucharist	87
Following Church teachings	86
Learning more about Catholic teaching and spirituality	82
Attending Mass	80
Participating in devotions such as Eucharistic Adoration or praying the Rosary	78

CATHOLICS AND POLITICS IN THE UNITED STATES

Catholics have played an important role in U.S. politics since the founding of the nation. Catholics took on an even greater political significance as they began to constitute a sizeable portion of the population in a number of key urban areas and states during the late nineteenth century. During the 1930s, Catholics formed a key component of the New Deal coalition that has made the Democratic party an important player and mobilizer of votes in American politics since.

In the late twentieth century, Catholics have come to be recognized as a critical swing vote that can determine the outcome of national as well as local elections. Catholics are somewhat more likely to vote than other citizens, and have provided nearly 30 percent of the votes in recent national elections. The fact that Catholics are concentrated in the largest and most electorally volatile states further contributes to their electoral significance, especially at the presidential level.

Catholic Political Identification

Catholic political identification patterns have often been attributed to the social and demographic characteristics of Catholics. In particular, factors associated with their relatively recent immigration, low socioeconomic status, and identity as members of a religious minority have been used to explain Catholic political preferences.

Political analysts have assumed that Catholics supported the Democratic party, its candidates, and its policies largely out of self-interest. They also predicted that Catholic allegiance to the Democratic party would decline as their socioeconomic status improved and they became more assimilated into the American social and cultural mainstream.   Other observers contended that Catholic commitment to the Democratic party was reinforced by the hierarchical structure of their church and the strong communal and associational ties within their communities.   The assumption was that Catholics were told to vote Democratic and that Catholic networks were used to help get out the vote.

The association between Catholics and the Democratic party, the party identified with the immigrant and the outsider, dates back to the mid-nineteenth century.   This relationship was strengthened in the early twentieth century with the campaign of Al Smith in 1928, the Democratic governor of New York who was the first Catholic to be nominated as a major party presidential candidate, and the New Deal realignment in 1932. For the next several decades, Catholics were a dependable component of the New Deal coalition and routinely provided a large share of the Democratic vote in elections at all levels.   During this period, Catholics retained many of the characteristics associated with Democratic party identification: working class, relatively low education, and residence in urban ethnic enclaves.

Although the socioeconomic characteristics of Catholics began to change by the 1950s, their expected mass movement toward the Republican party did not happen in the 1960s, which may have been a result of the intensification of ties to the Democratic party fostered by the campaign and election of John F. Kennedy in 1960. A visible degree of blue-collar, Catholic support for Republican platforms, or "Nixon Democrats," did emerge at this time.

By the 1970s, more Catholics began to exhibit changes in their political preferences. They became more conservative in certain attitudes and less reliably Democratic in their party identification and especially in their voting behavior. In the 1980s, Catholic movement toward the Republican party continued, particularly at the presidential level where Catholics formed a significant component of the "Reagan Democrats."

These shifts in Catholic attitudes, party identification, and voting choice toward more conservative and Republican directions signaled the long anticipated shift of Catholics from the Democratic party that many predicted would be the inevitable result of Catholic cultural assimilation and upward mobility. Nonetheless, Catholic loyalty to the Democratic party has remained relatively high throughout the second half of the twentieth century, particularly in comparison to Protestants and especially white Protestants. Whether measured in terms of voting, party identification, or attitudes on political issues, Catholics continue to be the most Democratic group of white Christians.

The comparisons of the percentage of Catholic and Protestant votes going to the Democratic, Republican, and independent candidates for president are shown in Table 2.4.

Table 2.4. The Catholic Vote for President: Democratic (D), Republican (R), and Independent (I) Candidates

	Catholic Voters			Protestant Voters		
	D	**R**	**I**	**D**	**R**	**I**
1948	65%	35%		45%	55%	
1952	51	49		33	67	
1956	45	55		34	66	
1960	82	18		34	66	
1964	78	22		58	42	
1968	55	37	8%	26	60	14%
1972	37	63		24	76	
1976	56	44		40	60	
1980	40	51	9	31	61	7
1984	44	56		28	72	
1988	52	48		33	67	
1992	48	29	22 Ross	34	47	19
1996	55	38	7 Perot	42	50	8

The persistent difference between Catholic and Protestant support for the Democratic presidential candidate is depicted in Figure 2.3 below. Although the Catholic vote and the Protestant vote have both fluctuated a great deal, the graph shows a consistent and sizeable gap between the two. Regardless of the election or the candidates presented, a consistently higher percentage of Catholics (solid line) than Protestants (dotted line) vote for the Democratic candidate, suggesting more continuity than discontinuity in party loyalty over the past 50 years.

In the early 1990s, Catholic identification with the Democratic party and Catholic votes for Democratic candidates in non-presidential elections continued to decline, and in 1994 a majority of Catholics voted for Republican candidates for Congress for the first time. However, these trends did not translate into significant increases in identification with the Republican party as much as a continued weakening of identification with the Democratic party.

Moreover, by the end of the decade, the decline in Democratic party identification among Catholics seems to have leveled off and may even be

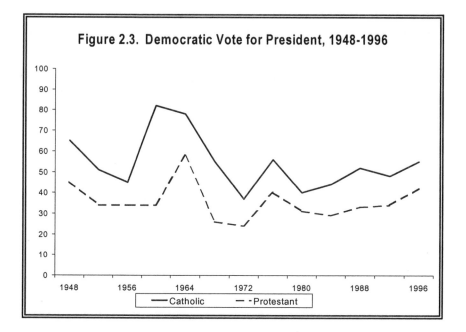

Figure 2.3. Democratic Vote for President, 1948-1996

reversing. Recent surveys indicate that at least a plurality of Catholics still identify with the Democratic party.   When "independent leaners" ("independent Democrats" and "independent Republicans" in Table 2.5 below) are included with party "identifiers," a majority of Catholics express a preference for the Democratic party.

Catholic Social and Political Attitudes
   On most political issues, Catholics tend to be more liberal than Protestants from both the mainline and evangelical traditions and more

Table 2.5. Catholic Party Identification
Percent of Catholics identifying with each

	1950s	1960s	1970s	1980s	1990s
Strong Democrat	28%	28%	20%	20%	20%
Weak Democrat	27	29	30	24	23
Independent Democrat	11	11	14	12	13
Independent	9	10	13	12	10
Independent Republican	6	5	8	11	13
Weak Republican	11	10	9	12	13
Strong Republican	8	6	6	9	9

Nixon strategy
didn't work

conservative than Jews and those with no religious affiliation.[7] The only real exception to this pattern is the issue of abortion, where Catholics are consistently found to be more opposed to abortion than mainline Protestants, though they are less opposed than evangelicals. These patterns hold for those at analogous levels of commitment and religious practice for each religious tradition.

Unlike Protestants, however, Catholics with socially conservative attitudes on such issues as gay rights, school prayer, and abortion are not significantly more likely to identify with the Republican party. Contrary to predictions by many analysts of the "culture wars," Catholics have not become part of a "traditionalist" coalition of social conservatives to any significant degree. Perhaps because they regard other issues, such as social welfare, support for the needy, and greater social tolerance – issues traditionally associated with the Democratic party – as also important, Catholics have maintained at least a marginal preference for the Democratic party in identification and voting choice. Moreover, even among Catholics who identify with and vote for the Republican party, there is a tendency to be more liberal on issues involving help for the needy and respect for the rights of others than is the case among their fellow political partisans from other religious traditions.

Table 2.6 shows the ideological self-placement of Catholics on different types of issues. These data, from the CARA Catholic Poll 2000, suggest that Catholics make distinctions among economic, social welfare, and social or moral issues. They are most likely to report that they are conservative on "social or moral issues like abortion" and least likely to say they are conservative "when it comes to social welfare programs that help the poor and needy." On social welfare issues as well as on "economic issues that involve taxing and spending," fairly large percentages identify themselves as moderate.

Table 2.6. Ideology and Political Issues among Catholics			
	Liberal	**Moderate**	**Conservative**
Economic issues	24%	37%	39%
Social welfare issues	31	40	29
Social or moral issues	32	25	42

Table 2.7, also taken from the CARA Catholic Poll 2000, shows the percent of Catholics who identify various issues as "very important." These findings suggest that Catholics consider social welfare issues and

moral issues to be much more important than economic issues, or at least those involving allowing businesses to operate more freely.

Table 2.7. Salience of Political Issues	
Percent of Catholics saying each is "very important"	
Government programs to help the needy	69%
Changing the moral direction of American culture	63
Reducing government regulations to allow businesses to operate more freely	40

The Catholic Imagination

One of the keys to understanding the persistent political differences between Catholics and members of other religious traditions may lie in what can be called the "Catholic imagination," the "Catholic ethic," or the "Catholic worldview." Certain tendencies among Catholics, such as their relatively liberal views on social welfare issues or their relatively conservative views on certain moral issues, may be at least partly the result of their underlying orientations and values rather than simply due to their social and demographic characteristics, or even political partisanship upon which social scientists have tended to focus.

Catholic theology and social teachings could well be expected to inculcate principles and values of humanitarian responsibility in the hearts and minds of believers. Presumably, these faith-based values and orientations can affect the political preferences of citizens and the way in which they approach social, moral, and political issues. At least some of the political distinctiveness of Catholics may be due to their religious faith, the images that characterize their religious imagination, and the ethical framework fostered by their religious tradition.

There is indeed evidence that suggests that Catholic attitudes and behaviors on a variety of social and political issues are distinctive because they have a more "sacramental" imagination and a more "communalistic" ethic than followers of other religious traditions. Research on the influence of the "Catholic imagination" is associated with the work of Andrew Greeley, a sociologist who is also a priest of the Archdiocese of Chicago. Based in part on the work of anthropologist Clifford Geertz and theologian David Tracy as well as survey research from the General Social Surveys, Greeley contends that there are distinctive Catholic and Protestant imaginations. Because of their distinctive imagination, Catholics tend to view God, the world, and human nature in more positive and "graceful" terms than Protestants. Greeley finds that these views influence Catholic attitudes on a range of social and political issues.

In a similar vein, sociologist and social policy expert John Tropman has argued that there is a distinctive "Catholic ethic" that parallels the more famous Protestant ethic. Whereas the Protestant ethic is oriented toward work, wealth, and achievement, the Catholic ethic is oriented toward sharing and helping others, especially the poor and disadvantaged.

To test these hypotheses, recent research builds upon the foundation laid by Greeley, Tropman, and others. The questions used by Greeley from the General Social Survey ask respondents to indicate whether there is "much goodness in the world which hints at God's goodness" or whether the

Table 2.8. The "Catholic Imagination": Differences in Worldview between Protestants and Catholics

	Catholic	Protestant	Difference
World filled with goodness	70%	47%	23%
Human nature basically good	70	47	23

"world is basically filled with evil" and whether "human nature is basically good" or if "human nature is fundamentally perverse and corrupt." Catholics tend to select responses consistent with an affirmation of the goodness of creation and a positive sense of human nature. CARA research supports the findings of Greeley and others that the "Catholic imagination" and "Catholic ethic" influence the political attitudes and behaviors of Catholics. The differences between Catholics and Protestants remain, even after controlling for the various social and demographic factors commonly used to explain Catholic attitudes and behaviors.[8]

Table 2.9. Differences between Protestants and Catholics: Support for Government Action

	Catholic	Protestant	Difference
To help the poor	74%	65%	9%
To help the sick	81	73	8
To help blacks	49	40	9
To foster active government	67	54	13

These differences between Catholics and Protestants, perhaps stemming from the sacramental and communal dimensions of Catholicism, seem to reflect a different intuition about social institutions and social problems. In any case, Catholics are also significantly more likely to see government as a positive force that can help the poor, sick, and others, as shown in Table 2.9.

CONCLUSION

Catholics in the United States were once distinguished for a high level of religious practice that reflected a strong and largely self-contained culture. Today, Catholic attendance figures have declined to the point that they are about the same as other religious groups. Yet despite these changes, Catholic attitudes and political identification remain distinctive, suggesting a persistence of deep-seated differences in worldview between Protestants and Catholics.

The impact of Catholic identity and its influence on attitudes and behaviors is independent of demographic or socioeconomic contexts. Rates of participation in rituals and sacraments are relatively similar across different locations, ethnic backgrounds and social classes. The religious identity of Catholics seem rooted in a shared Catholic culture, expressed through traditions and individual practice, and nurtured in Catholic institutional life. This shared culture helps to unify U.S. Catholics into a single Church that maintains a distinctive worldview.

As the data demonstrate, maintaining Catholic values in political and social contexts is a role taken on by all Catholics. Nonetheless, Catholic institutions have a special responsibility in passing on that tradition. The remainder of the book examines trends in Catholic institutional life and personnel, two key elements that lend support to Catholics as they build and pass on their faith.

PART II

Changes and Continuities in Catholic Institutions

Catholicism places great emphasis on a communal approach to faith. This means that Catholics instinctively turn to institutional and organizational life as a means of maintaining unity and passing on a common faith. Indeed, this may help explain in part how Catholicism successfully maintained its unity in the United States in spite of its diverse membership and the denominationally based Protestant model that has been part of U.S. culture from the nation's beginnings.

As in any religious context, Catholic life and culture are passed on through networks of family, friends, and associates. For Catholics, these relationships are mediated, and the faith cultivated and expressed, in Catholic institutions. The most formal are those organized and controlled territorially under diocesan bishops who act as their chief shepherd. The word "diocese" originally referred to a unit of the Roman Empire and has been used in the West since the earliest centuries of Christianity to name the specific territorial responsibility of the presiding bishop.

Catholic institutions range from formal schools that provide for the education and formation of the young to the somewhat less institutionally oriented parish religious education programs. They range from campaigns that gather the local Catholic community in support of their Church and each other to efforts to provide health care, promote justice, and generally serve the needs of the entire community without regard to religious expression or commitment.

The second part of this portrait of Catholicism in the United States examines the formal organizations of Catholic life and how they have changed over the centuries. It looks at key institutions in which Catholics structure their lives as church members, starting with the local faith community.

Chapter 3 describes the basic organization of Catholic life in the United States, examining crucial aspects of diocesan and parish life today as well as relevant statistical trends.

Chapter 4 shows trends in Catholic education, including schools and religious education and formation programs. This chapter gives an overview of Catholic elementary schools, high schools, and colleges and universities. Over the past few decades, parish-related catechetical efforts outside of Catholic schools have come to play a leading role in religious education. These, too, represent "Catholic education."

Chapter 5 discusses Catholic health care and charitable agencies, representing Catholic efforts to alleviate suffering and serve the needs of the poor at home and abroad, including Catholic missionary work overseas. This chapter shows how Catholic organizations have changed over the past century – responding to pressures of specialization, professionalization, and centralization – while at the same time maintaining continuity with their Catholic identity and the broader Catholic community from which they rise.

CHAPTER 3

Dioceses and Parishes

In 1789, Baltimore became the first city in the present-day United States to be established as a Catholic diocesan see city, or the location of a bishop's residence and cathedral. At that time, some 35 priests served approximately 35,000 Catholics in the United States – less than one percent of the U.S. population. Of course, for at least 200 years before that time other parts of the present-day United States, particularly in the Spanish- and French-held areas, had long had flourishing centers of Catholic life.

By 1822, there were eight dioceses in the U.S., organizing

Table 3.1. Growth of Dioceses and Parishes in the United States

	Dioceses/ Eparchies*	Parishes	Catholics	Percent of U.S. Population
1800	1	35	35,000	1%
1850	27	1,073	1,606,000	8
1900	86	6,409	10,774,989	14
1950	125	15,533	28,634,878	19
1998	192	19,181	59,156,237	22

*An "eparchy" is the equivalent of "diocese" for the Eastern Churches of the Catholic Church in the United States.

approximately 200 parishes for more than 250,000 Catholics. By 1850, Catholic churches could be found in every state and territory. Table 3.1 illustrates the remarkable growth in dioceses and parishes that began early in the nineteenth century and continues to the present time.[1] Maps in the Appendix trace out the growth in dioceses in the United States since the beginning of its history.

ECCLESIAL STRUCTURE

The Catholic Church in the United States is led by the bishops and eparchs of the 192 Catholic dioceses and eparchies that belong to the United States Conference of Catholic Bishops (USCCB).[2]

These 192 dioceses and eparchies are grouped into 33 ecclesiastical provinces, each of which is led by an archdiocese or archeparchy. Two of these provinces are for the Eastern Churches: one for the Ruthenian Church and another for the Ukrainian Church. The other Eastern Churches (Maronite, Melkite, Armenian, Chaldean, Syrian, and the Armenian Exarchate) are immediately subject to the Holy See in Rome and do not belong to any of the 33 U.S. provinces. Due to its special character, the Military Archdiocese is the only archdiocese in the U.S. that does not serve as a metropolitan or principal diocese for an ecclesiastical province; it oversees Catholic military personnel wherever U.S. armed forces serve, at home or abroad.

Table 3.2. Dioceses and Eparchies in the United States			
Latin Rite		**Eastern Churches**	
Archdioceses	32	Archeparchies	2
Dioceses	145	Eparchies	13

Regions of the United States Conference of Catholic Bishops (USCCB)

First established in 1966, and reorganized periodically since then, these regions group all dioceses and eparchies whose bishops or eparchs belong to the USCCB into one of 13 regions, based on the location of the see city.

The USCCB regions sometimes cut across ecclesiastical provinces or states, in cases where geographic, cultural, or logistical considerations are more relevant than the boundaries of ecclesiastical provinces or states. Regions XI and XIII include parts of the ecclesiastical province of San

Table 3.3. USCCB Regions, by Territory and Ecclesiastical Provinces

Region I
New England
States of CT, ME, MA, NH, RI, and VT
Provinces of Boston and Hartford

Region II
New York
State of NY
Province of New York

Region III
Mid Atlantic
States of NJ and PA
Provinces of Newark and Philadelphia

Region IV
South Atlantic
States of DE, FL, GA, MD, NC, SC, VA, WV, the District of Columbia, Military Archdiocese, and the U.S. Virgin Islands. Provinces of Atlanta, Baltimore, Miami, and Washington

Region V
South Central
States of AL, KY, LA, MS, and TN
Provinces of Louisville, Mobile, New Orleans

Region VI
Eastern Midwest
States of MI and OH
Provinces of Cincinnati and Detroit

Region VII
Upper Midwest
States of IL, IN, and WI
Provinces of Chicago, Indianapolis, and Milwaukee

Region VIII
Upper Plains
States of MN, ND, and SD
Province of Saint Paul-Minneapolis

Region IX
Central Plains
States of IA, KS, MO, and NE
Provinces of Dubuque, Kansas City in Kansas, Omaha, and Saint Louis

Region X
Lower Plains
States of AR, OK, and TX (except El Paso)
Provinces of Oklahoma City and San Antonio

Region XI
Pacific
States of CA, HI, and NV
Province of Los Angeles and the Province of San Francisco (except the Diocese of Salt Lake City)

Region XII
Northwest
States of AK, ID, MT, OR, and WA
Provinces of Anchorage, Portland, and Seattle

Region XIII
Mountain
States of UT, AZ, NM, CO, WY, part of TX
Provinces of Denver and Santa Fe (includes the Diocese of El Paso) and part of the Province of San Francisco (the Diocese of Salt Lake City)

St. Thomas in the U.S. Virgin Islands, which had some eight parishes and 11 diocesan priests in 1998, is also not included in the table.

Table 3.5. Characteristics of the Episcopal Conference Regions for Dioceses and Archdioceses in the United States*

USCCB Region	Dioceses	Catholics	Percent Catholic	Priests	Parishes	Size in 1,000 mi.^{2}
I	11	5,653,534	42%	4,870	1,656	66.7
II	8	7,347,611	40%	5,236	1,669	49.0
III	13	6,896,305	35%	5,916	2,001	53.1
IV	18	4,674,623	10%	4,480	1,560	275.2
V	18	2,102,858	10%	2,232	1,175	229.0
VI	13	4,417,487	21%	3,648	1,731	99.9
VII	16	6,123,618	27%	5,603	2,391	148.7
VIII	10	1,418,525	25%	1,367	1,058	232.2
IX	15	2,117,499	17%	2,969	1,643	285.6
X	16	4,501,029	18%	2,238	1,181	363.3
XI	15	9,599,463	27%	3,934	1,187	275.2
XII	11	1,276,143	11%	1,337	655	547.9
XIII	11	2,478,539	18%	1,505	676	547.4
TOTAL	175	58,607,234	22%	45,335	18,563	3,615.3

*These numbers do not include the Eastern Churches

The New York Region (II), for example, includes just eight dioceses in the State of New York but has the densest population in terms of Catholics per square mile. It ranks second in Catholic population and number of parishes and third in number of priests, including both religious and diocesan. In contrast, the Northwest Region (XII), which includes Washington, Oregon, Montana, Idaho, and Alaska, has only two Catholics per square mile, 655 widely dispersed parishes, and fewer total priests than any other region.

In terms of Catholics per parish, as shown in Table 3.6, the Pacific Region (XI) averages 8,087 Catholics per parish, nearly twice as many as the New York Region (II), with 4,402. The Central Plains Region (IX) has the fewest Catholics per parish (1,289). Similarly, the greatest territorial

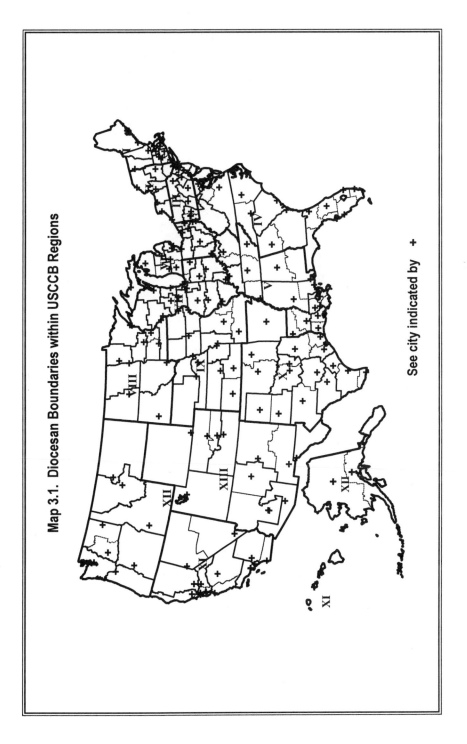

Map 3.1. Diocesan Boundaries within USCCB Regions

See city indicated by +

size of parishes (given as the average size of parishes in square miles) is to be found in the two westernmost regions, the Northwest Region (XII) and the Mountain Region (XIII). Each is more than twice as large as parishes in other regions. However, those two regions are also the least densely populated with Catholics. The Northwest Region (XII) has only two Catholics per square mile, and the Mountain Region (XIII) has five Catholics per square mile. The most densely Catholic regions are the New York Region (II) and Mid Atlantic Region (III) in the Northeast.

USCCB Region	Catholics per Parish	Square Miles per Parish	Catholics per Square Mile
I	3,414	40	85
II	4,402	29	150
III	3,446	27	130
IV	2,993	177	17
V	1,790	195	9
VI	2,552	58	44
VII	2,583	63	41
VIII	1,341	219	6
IX	1,289	174	7
X	3,811	308	12
XI	8,087	232	35
XII	1,948	836	2
XIII	3,666	810	5

Table 3.6. Average Number of Catholics and Parish Size by USCCB Region

ARCHDIOCESES AND DIOCESES, ARCHEPARCHIES AND EPARCHIES

The primary structural unit of Church life is the diocese or eparchy, which is a grouping of parishes organized into a "particular" church (the term used in the Church's basic juridical framework, the Code of Canon Law) under the jurisdiction of a diocesan bishop or eparch.[6]

An archdiocese is the "metropolitan" or "principal" diocese of an ecclesiastical province, or group of dioceses. Typically, the archdiocese is the historic "mother" diocese from which others were created, and is usually, but not necessarily, the largest in its ecclesiastical province. Population may have changed over time to the point that neighboring dioceses are larger. For example, Table 3.7 below lists the Diocese of Galveston-Houston as the tenth largest by Catholic population. The diocese is part of the Province of San Antonio, but has more Catholics than the Archdiocese of San Antonio. Two other dioceses that rank among the ten largest in the U.S. are Brooklyn and Rockville Center, both of which are part of the Province of New York. In fact, the Diocese of Brooklyn shares New York City with the Archdiocese of New York. If the Archdiocese of New York were to encompass the entire city, it would be almost exactly as big as the largest archdiocese in the United States, Los Angeles.

Table 3.7. The Ten Largest Dioceses by Catholic Population	
Diocese or Archdiocese	**Catholics**
Archdiocese of Los Angeles	4,080,793
Archdiocese of New York	2,371,355
Archdiocese of Chicago	2,358,000
Archdiocese of Boston	2,042,688
Diocese of Brooklyn	1,625,547
Archdiocese of Detroit	1,453,756
Archdiocese of Philadelphia	1,411,256
Diocese of Rockville Centre	1,359,432
Archdiocese of Newark	1,319,558
Diocese of Galveston-Houston	906,330

The average number of Catholics per diocese is 335,574. As Table 3.8 shows, however, many archdioceses and dioceses are larger, while many are significantly smaller than this average. Half of all dioceses in the United States have more, and half fewer, than 185,000 Catholics.

Mid-size dioceses in the United States range from 125,000 to about 225,000 Catholics. There are 33 dioceses in this range, and they make up some 17 percent of all dioceses. Mid-size dioceses are primarily urban or suburban in composition and are often near a larger, more urban diocese (such as Monterey, between Los Angeles and San Francisco, or Wilmington, between Baltimore and Philadelphia). Table 3.8 shows the percent of all dioceses that are very large, mid-sized, and very small in terms of their Catholic population.

Table 3.8. Dioceses and Eparchies by Catholic Population*

Population	Number	Percent
Very Large: Over 1,000,000 Catholics	9	5%
Large: 225,000 - 999,999 Catholics	65	34
Mid-size: 125,000 - 224,999 Catholics	33	17
Small: 40,000 - 124,999 Catholics	66	35
Fewer than 40,000 Catholics	17	9
TOTAL	190	100

*This table covers territorially based dioceses and eparchies within the fifty states and District of Columbia. Hence, the Military Archdiocese and the Diocese of the U.S. Virgin Islands are excluded.

The newest Latin Rite diocese is the Diocese of Las Vegas, established in 1995. It has a Catholic population of 390,000, but only 24 parishes, for an average of 16,250 persons per parish.

Percent Catholic

Nearly ten percent of dioceses and eparchies in the United States, 17 in all, have fewer than 40,000 Catholics. Eleven of those 17 ecclesiastical

---

Table 3.9. The Ten Dioceses with the Highest Percent of Catholics Relative to the Total Population

	Percent Catholic
Brownsville, Texas	85%
El Paso, Texas	76
Houma-Thibodaux, Louisiana	65
Providence, Rhode Island	64
Lafayette, Louisiana	60
Boston, Massachusetts	54
Newark, New Jersey	50
Fall River, Massachusetts	47
Rockville Centre, New York	47
Buffalo, New York	47

jurisdictions are eparchies. Others are very extensive, with their population spread out over sparsely settled areas. Two such dioceses are in Alaska, with well below one Catholic per square mile. The Diocese of Rapid City, South Dakota, with 35,605 Catholics, has one Catholic per square mile. The Diocese of Baker, Oregon, with 35,558 Catholics, has one Catholic every two square miles.

Relative to the number of non-Catholics, the Diocese of Brownsville, Texas, has the most concentrated Catholic population, some 85 percent of the population is Catholic.[7] Six of the ten dioceses with the highest percentage of Catholics are in the Northeast, a traditional center of Catholic population. But four of these are in the South – two in Texas (Brownsville and El Paso) and two in Louisiana (Houma-Thibodaux and Lafayette). In contrast, the Diocese of Knoxville, Tennessee, has the lowest proportion of Catholics in the population of any U.S. diocese: two percent.[8]

Catholics per Parish

Another helpful way to compare different kinds of dioceses is to examine the average number of Catholics per parish within each diocese. This figure ranges from a low of 356 Catholics per parish in the Diocese of Fairbanks, Alaska, to a high of over 16,000 Catholics per parish in the Diocese of Las Vegas. Nearly 40 percent of all dioceses and eparchies average at least 2,500 Catholics per parish.

Table 3.10. Average Parish Size by Diocese or Eparchy		
Average Catholics per Parish	**Number**	**Percent**
Fewer than 1,000	39	20%
1,000 - 1,499	34	18
1,500 - 2,499	47	25
2,500 - 8,000	62	33
More than 8,000	9	5

PARISHES

According to the CARA National Parish Inventory there are approximately 19,181 Catholic parishes in the 50 states and the District of Columbia. In 1950, there were 15,295 parishes in that same area. Therefore, the number of Catholic parishes increased by 3,886, or 25 percent, over the last half of the twentieth century. Catholic population in that same territory, on the other hand, has grown by some 106 percent since who are registered are not regular attenders. Also, parishes that maintain registration information on a family basis frequently list both spouses of a religiously mixed marriage on the lists, even though only one person may actually be Catholic.[10]

Parish Seating Capacity
    The typical Catholic parish church is designed to seat approximately 500 people.

Table 3.14. Parish Church Seating Capacity

Largest 25 percent of parish churches	650 - 3,000
Second largest 25 percent of parish churches	430 - 649
Second smallest 25 percent of parish churches	300 - 429
Smallest 25 percent of parish churches	30 - 299

Since half of all parish churches accommodate fewer than 430 persons at a time, it is not surprising that most parishes celebrate multiple Sunday Masses. The average number of Masses is 3.5 per weekend, including Saturday Vigil and Sunday Masses. However, ten percent of parishes have only one Mass, while five percent have as many as seven or more. Depending on the location, in the case of small numbers of Masses, this may be a reflection of few clergy available to preside at Mass, or of few parishioners. In the case of a large number of Masses, this may reflect a very large parish population, or the local parish's ability to respond to the needs of its Catholic population.

Table 3.15. Number of Saturday Vigil and Sunday Masses

Masses Celebrated	Percent of all Parishes
Five or more	25%
Four	21
Three	28
Two	16
One	10

Metropolitan and Non-metropolitan Parishes
    Approximately 80 percent of people in the United States live in metropolitan areas as defined by the U.S. Bureau of the Census. This term

describes counties with a central place of at least 50,000 persons or an urbanized area with a total population of at least 100,000, which includes both urban and suburban areas. About 64 percent of parishes in the United States are located in metropolitan areas that together comprise 21 percent of U.S. territory. Slightly more than a third of parishes are in the areas designated non-metropolitan by the U.S. Census, having a central place of fewer than 50,000 persons or an urban center of fewer than 100,000 persons.[11] Table 3.16 describes typical characteristics of parishes located in metropolitan and non-metropolitan areas. While parish size is probably the most apparent and expected difference, metropolitan and non-metropolitan parishes also differ in many other aspects.

Table 3.16. Average Characteristics of Metropolitan and Non-metropolitan Area Parishes

	Metropolitan Parishes	Non-metropolitan Parishes	All Parishes
Households	1,070	387	843
Seating capacity	559	344	500
Masses per weekend	4	3	3.5
Ratio of baptisms to funerals	2.8	2.1	2.5
Percent with resident pastor	94%	84%	91%
Priests (including part time)	1.9	1.3	1.7
Deacons	1.8	1.4	1.7
Lay staff	4.3	3.4	4.1
Percent identified Hispanic/Latino	19%	13%	13%
Percent identified Black	2.6%	0.4%	7%
Percent identified Asian	1.3%	0.3%	2%

Differences between parishes in metropolitan and non-metropolitan areas include the following:

- Metropolitan parishes average more than 2.75 times the number of registered families than non-metropolitan parishes, but their churches have the capacity to hold only 1.5 times as many parishioners.

- Metropolitan parishes average more Masses per weekend to accommodate their parishioners.

- A higher percentage of metropolitan parishes than non-metropolitan parishes say they minister to Hispanics/Latinos, to African Americans, or to Asians.

Table 3.17. Parish Characteristics and Parish Size

Very Large Parishes (More than 3,000 registered parishioners)
91 Percent located in "metropolitan" areas
2.9 Ratio of baptisms to funerals
21 Percent are identified Hispanic/Latino parishes
100 Percent have a resident pastor
2.3 Average number of priests per parish
5.3 Average number of lay professional staff

Large Parishes (From 1,200 to 3,000 registered parishioners)
75 Percent located in "metropolitan" areas
2.6 Ratio of baptisms to funerals
20 Percent are identified Hispanic/Latino parishes
97 Percent have a resident pastor
1.6 Average number of priests per parish
4   Average number of lay professional staff

Mid-size Parishes (From 450 to 1,200 registered parishioners)
56 Percent located in "metropolitan" areas
2.3 Ratio of baptisms to funerals
16 Percent are identified Hispanic/Latino parishes
90 Percent have a resident pastor
1.4 Average number of priests per parish
3.2 Average number of lay professional staff

Small Parishes (Fewer than 450 registered parishioners)
37 Percent located in "metropolitan" areas
2.1 Ratio of baptisms to funerals
11 Percent are identified Hispanic/Latino parishes
74 Percent have a resident pastor
1.3 Average number of priests per parish
2.5 Average number of lay professional staff

Characteristics of Parishes according to Size

As Table 3.17 shows, parish size also affects parish life. Parish characteristics differ dramatically by number of registered parishioners. The four divisions used here represent approximately one-fourth each of all parishes in the United States.[12] Comparing parishes by relative size, Table 3.17 shows:

- All very large parishes have a resident pastor, while more than one in four small parishes lack a resident pastor.

- More than nine in ten very large parishes are in metropolitan areas but just over a third of small parishes are in metropolitan areas.

- Very large parishes average three baptisms for every funeral, suggesting a strongly positive growth rate and a younger population for these parishes.[13] On the other hand, small parishes have an average of two baptisms for every funeral, suggesting positive growth, but at a slower rate. Nationally, parishes average 2.5 infant baptisms for each funeral. Seventy percent of parishes have more infant baptisms than funerals.

- Identified Hispanic/Latino parishes (those parishes with a majority of Hispanic/Latino parishioners or an identified ministry to Hispanics/Latinos) are more likely to be large or very large parishes. Only one in ten small parishes has an identified Hispanic/Latino ministry.

- Professional lay staff and priests per parish increase with parish size.

Non-English Language Masses

On average, one in five parishes celebrates two Sunday Masses in a language other than English each week. Most frequently, that language is Spanish. About 70 percent of parishes that report non-English language Masses have at least one Mass a month in Spanish. Nearly one in six diocesan priests, and about a third of religious priests in parochial ministry say they use Spanish in their ministry.

Ethnic Diversity and Parish Life

Since the first German-language parish was created in Philadelphia in 1787, the Catholic Church in the United States has included language or ethnically based parishes as an important organizing feature for local faith communities.

Over the past few decades, however, as European ethnic populations assimilated into mainstream American culture and their children moved into the suburbs, these older, largely urban ethnic parishes have dwindled in members, changed in ethnic composition, and some have closed.

During this same period, Catholic thinking about parish life has increasingly valued transcending national or cultural boundaries. Dioceses today are less likely to specifically establish or promote national or language-specific parishes to minister to particular cultural or language groups. A single parish today often contains a diversity of ethnic groups.

As a result, many parishes provide pastoral ministry to a broad ethnic mix of Catholics within their parish boundaries. Nevertheless, sometimes

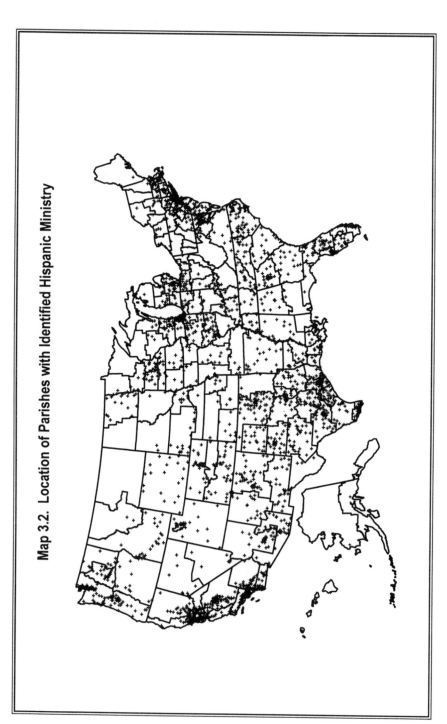

Map 3.2. Location of Parishes with Identified Hispanic Ministry

simply identifying these groups can be a serious challenge. Dioceses have not traditionally asked parishes to identify ethnic subgroups in a single parish (as opposed to a "national" parish where ethnicity is central to parish identity).

Some parishes do identify with one (and in some cases more than one) nationality or ethnic identity. For some parishes, this identity is rooted in the neighborhood population they serve at present or served historically. For those founded as personal parishes to meet the needs of a certain nationality or ethnic group, this parish identity is their organizing principle and the basis of membership and participation. Not all parishes with a single large, predominant ethnic culture or nationality, however, identify themselves in this way. Therefore this is an incomplete measure of parish

Table 3.18. Parish-Reported Ethnicity or Nationality
(May include multiple ethnic identities for a single parish)

Ethnic/National Identification	Percent
Hispanic, Latino, Mexican, Dominican, Puerto Rican, etc.	21%
Polish or Polish and another identification	15
German or German and another identification	13
Slovak, Lithuanian, Hungarian, Czech, or other Central or Eastern Europe	11
Italian or Italian and another identification	10
African American, African, or African American and another identification	7
Irish or Irish and another identification	6
French, French Canadian, or French and another identification	4
Native American, or a specific Native American tribe	3
Spanish, Basque, or Spanish and another identification	2
Filipino or Filipino and another identification	1
Vietnamese, Hmong, Laotian	1
Lebanese, Maronite, Arabic	1

cultural identity. Table 3.18 shows the most common identities expressed by the approximately one in six parishes that associate themselves with a particular ethnic group or nationality.[14]

Parish Racial and Ethnic Composition

Of parishes that report the racial/ethnic composition of the parish, the breakdown is as follows:

- Eighty-nine percent say their parish is more than 40 percent white.

- Eight percent say the parish is more than 40 percent African American or of African descent.

- Another 14 percent say their parish is more than 40 percent Hispanic/Latino.

- Nearly 3 percent report the parish is more than 40 percent Asian.

- About 1 percent report their parish is more than 40 percent American Indian/Native American.

Table 3.19. Average Characteristics of Parishes with Identities, Ministries, or Populations Greater than 40 percent for Each Group

	White	Hispanic/ Latino	African American	Asian	Native American
Households	872	1,031	447	1,080	312
Seating capacity	484	540	486	589	281
Masses per weekend	3.5	4.3	2.7	4.4	2.4
Metropolitan location	68%	72%	92%	87%	26%
Infants baptized	43	91	24	74	28
Funerals per year	27	32	15	33	19
Baptism/Funeral ratio	1.6	4.3	1.8	2.9	2.3
Confirmations yearly	39	44	18	43	17
Marriages per year	14	23	8	28	4
Priests	1.7	1.9	1.6	1.9	1.7
Deacons	1.4	13.7	1.3	1.6	1.5
Women Religious	1.6	1.7	1.5	1.9	2.3
Lay staff (excluding religious)	4.3	4.6	3.4	4.7	2.7

Table 3.19 compares parishes with identities, ministries, or populations greater than 40 percent for each major racial or ethnic group. Findings about parish life in these parishes include:

- Parishes of African Americans and Native Americans are more likely to be small (fewer than 450 registered parishioners), while parishes with ministries to Hispanics/Latinos and Asians are more likely to be large. On average, white parishes are neither as large as Hispanic/Latino or

Asian parishes nor as small as African American or Native American parishes.

- Parishes of African Americans and Native Americans tend to have smaller church buildings and celebrate just under three Masses per weekend. By contrast, parishes of Hispanics/Latinos and Asians have larger church buildings and celebrate about four Masses per weekend. Again, white parishes are in-between, with an average of 3.5 Masses.

- Native American parishes are mostly non-metropolitan. African American, Asian, Hispanic/Latino, and white parishes are usually located in metropolitan areas.

- Hispanic/Latino parishes have more than four baptisms for every funeral, suggesting that their parishioners are relatively younger.

- Parishes with ministry to Hispanics/Latinos and Asians have greater numbers of priests, deacons, and lay staff per parish, as well as higher average numbers participating in parish sacramental life. This is likely a function of the relatively larger size of these parishes.

Parish Staff

Parishes today are about a third larger than they were in the 1950s but are staffed by fewer priests. It is no longer common to have several priests serving one parish. Indeed, it is becoming more common now to have one pastor with responsibility for more than one parish. Of the more than 80 percent of parishes that have a resident priest pastor:

- 58 percent have a single priest serving the parish.

- 25 percent have two priests serving the parish.

- 17 percent have more than two priests.

Table 3.20. Priest Staffing in Parishes
Percent of parishes with resident pastors staffed by:

	Only One Priest	Two Priests	Three or More Priests
Diocesan Priests	65%	23%	12%
Religious Priests	66%	21%	13%

Priest staffing patterns are not affected by whether a parish is staffed by diocesan priests or under the administration of religious priests, as can be seen in Table 3.20.

Some 17 percent of all parishes are administered by non-resident pastors or entrusted to someone other than a priest.[15]

Table 3.21. Administration of Parishes without a Resident Pastor Number of parishes in each region:				
	Northeast	**South**	**Midwest**	**West**
Total parishes	5,700	4,138	7,027	2,526
Parish has a resident pastor	5,146	3,552	5,075	2,230
Administered by				
non-resident pastor	534	476	1,756	224
Entrusted to deacon	5	34	36	15
Entrusted to religious brother	1	6	4	1
Entrusted to woman religious	12	62	121	27
Entrusted to lay persons	2	8	35	29
TOTAL	554	586	1,952	296
Percent of all parishes	10%	14%	28%	12%

Findings relative to the administration of parishes without a resident pastor include the following:

- When there is not a priest available for assignment in a parish, the solution for nine in ten parishes in the Northeast is to assign a non-resident priest to administer the parish. This solution is next most frequently found in Midwestern parishes that have no resident pastor. Parishes in the South and the West are less likely to have a non-resident pastor in cases where insufficient priests are available.

- Twenty-eight percent of parishes in the Midwest have no resident pastor, the highest percentage of all five regions. Six percent of all parishes for which a non-resident pastor is not available are entrusted to women religious.

- The South and the West have deacons entrusted with the care of about six percent of parishes with no resident pastor.

- The South is also more likely to have parishes entrusted to women religious. More than ten percent of all parishes in the South with no resident pastor are entrusted to women religious.

- The West has the highest percentage of parishes entrusted to a lay person or team. About a tenth of parishes in the West with no resident pastor are entrusted to lay persons other than vowed religious.

Ministry staff of parishes is comprised of deacons and ecclesial lay ministers, including vowed religious, as well as priests. Table 3.22 shows average parish ministry staff by region, illustrating differences across regions and between lay and ordained staff.

Table 3.22. Average Parish Ministry Staff by Region (Includes both full-time and part-time ministers)				
	Northeast	**South**	**Midwest**	**West**
Diocesan priests	1.04	.69	.83	.69
Religious priests	.24	.25	.19	.23
Deacons	.31	.34	.33	.22
Religious brothers	.02	.03	.03	.02
Religious sisters	.34	.25	.28	.23

More than nine in ten parishes also report having a parish pastoral council, although council members are not considered ministry staff. Though not required by canon law, a parish pastoral council is recommended "if the diocesan bishop considers it opportune" (canon 536). The pastoral council serves as a consultative body to the pastor.

CONCLUSION

A detailed look at dioceses and parish structures reveals the great geographic, demographic, and cultural diversity of Catholicism in the United States. There are 177 dioceses, 14 eparchies, and one exarchate with bishops, eparchs and one exarch belong to the United States Conference of Catholic Bishops. These are organized into 33 provinces and 13 regions. There are 34 archdioceses, of which 31 are metropolitan sees of ecclesiastical provinces for Latin Rite dioceses, two of which are metropolitan sees of ecclesiastical provinces for Eastern Church eparchies, and one is the Military Archdiocese.

Most dioceses have a relatively small Catholic population in comparison to the total population of the dioceses. Only two of the 13 USCCB Regions have dioceses where the Catholic population is 40 percent or more, while six have dioceses with Catholic populations of 20 percent or less. Some of the larger dioceses have exceptionally large Catholic populations. Eighteen dioceses have fewer than 40,000 Catholics, but nine have more than one million Catholics. Dioceses with the largest percentages of their population that is Catholic tend to be in the Northeast, though several are in Louisiana and Texas; dioceses with the lowest Catholic percentages tend to be in the Southeast, or a mountain state such as Utah.

Well over one-third of all parishes exceeds 2,500 registered parishioners. Almost all parishes with more than 3,000 registered parishioners have a resident pastor, but more than one in four small parishes lack a resident pastor. One-fifth of parishes in the U.S. celebrates a Mass in a language other than English. At least 70 percent of these parishes offer at least one Mass per month in Spanish.

The data demonstrate just how great these changes over time have been for many dioceses and parishes in the U.S. However, it is also clear that the Catholic Church in the U.S. has a structure that can adapt and change to shifts in population and availability of human and material resources.

CHAPTER 4

Catholic Education

Few trends are more directly related to the future of Catholic life in the United States than those that describe Catholic education. The Church broadly understands "education" to include parish elementary and secondary schools as well as parish-based education programs, Catholic colleges and universities, ministry programs at non-Catholic institutes of higher education, and seminaries and institutions for lay ministry formation. Debates continue regarding the Catholic identity of schools, their funding sources, and their accessibility, as well as the definition of education and educational institutions as a critical part of the Church's mission. However, Catholic education remains as important to the Church's life at the beginning of the twenty-first century as it was at the beginning of the twentieth.

THE EMERGENCE OF A CATHOLIC SCHOOL SYSTEM

Origins

The roots of most Catholic educational institutions in the United States were part of a strategy to pass on the faith to the next generation in the context of a relatively hostile surrounding culture. Exhortations from the Church hierarchy to educate children in Catholic institutions were reinforced by a widespread desire on the part of the laity to use formal education as the vehicle to transmit religious values and in some cases ethnic traditions, language, and other elements of their culture to their children. In the mid-nineteenth century, the Catholic educational system

63

quickly evolved into the second largest in the country after the public school system. Many of its institutions built up reputations as places of rigorous scholarship and intellectual training. Today, although Catholic education is less looked upon as a fortress from which to defend the faith, it is still one of the principal means by which Catholic learning and traditions are preserved and transmitted to younger generations.

Catholic schooling first came to the Americas as the Church expanded into the New World. The first universities of the New World were founded with ecclesiastical approval in Mexico and Peru in 1551, derived from missionary efforts to educate indigenous peoples and the first generations of youth born in the colonies. Farther north, the first permanent Catholic educational institution appeared in 1740, when Bohemia Manor was established by the Jesuits in Maryland to educate young men as potential candidates for the priesthood. This was the institutional foundation for today's Georgetown Preparatory School and Georgetown University, established in 1789. The Ursulines, a European teaching order,[1] founded the first academy for young women in present-day U.S. territory in New Orleans in 1727. The first founded on U.S. soil was Visitation Academy at Georgetown in 1799, still in operation today.

The first documented Catholic parish school was established in 1782 by St. Mary's Church in Philadelphia, then the city with the largest per capita population of Catholics (400 out of 18,000). At that time, however, very few parishes had sufficient resources to build churches, much less schools, for their parishioners. The great majority of Catholic parish schools opened afterward depended on the sacrifice and talent of vowed religious, mostly women, beginning with Elizabeth Seton's founding the Sisters of Charity and opening the first Catholic free school in Emmitsburg, Maryland, in 1809. In some cities and towns with mixed populations and in some frontier areas, local governments funded Catholic schools or invited religious orders to staff schools, just as they funded schools of the Protestant faiths to make up for the lack of public facilities.

The emergence of the public school movement, combined with a dramatic rise in the immigration of Catholics to the United States, galvanized interest in creating a more formalized parish school system. At the first Council of Baltimore in 1829, the bishops of the United States recommended the establishment of schools in connection with churches and permitted the use of parish funds to pay teachers. In the 1830s and 1840s, Catholic bishops continued to debate the merits of Catholic schools versus the acceptability of public schools for the education of Catholic children. This was the same time when state-supported, free public schools were being developed. However, these included a "common core" of religious education based on Protestant teachings and ethics as well as a curriculum intended to inculcate students into the practice of "American" traditions, which were often greatly influenced by Protestant, Anglo-Saxon traditions. This led to resentment and resistance on the part of Catholic laity and Church leadership alike.

Development

Over the next several decades, as the public school movement gained strength and courts ruled against public funding for religious education, the bishops began issuing stronger statements on behalf of Catholic schools. In 1858, the Second Provincial Council of Cincinnati mandated that all pastors build a parochial school under pain of mortal sin. In some parishes, pastors denied the sacraments to parents who did not send their children to Catholic schools, a practice reinforced by instructions sent from the Vatican in 1876. In 1884, the Third Plenary Council of Baltimore mandated the establishment of a school in every parish, the obligation of the pastor and of the parishioners to support the school, and the requirement that parents send their children to parochial schools. While individual Catholics would no longer be denied sacramental privileges if they did not comply, whole parishes could be put under interdict if the parishioners refused to support a parish school. In the words of Bishop Bernard McQuaid of Rochester, raising and strengthening the walls of the Catholic fortress by building Catholic schools would serve to protect children from the "wolves of the world" that were "destroying countless numbers of the unguarded ones."

Some prelates, such as Archbishop John Ireland of St. Paul, Minnesota, still felt that the Church should support cooperative efforts to have Catholic children educated by both the public school system and the parish, as part of the effort to integrate the Catholic faith more fully into American life. Years later these issues were resolved at the local level, in some areas resulting in released-time arrangements between parishes and local school boards.

Catholic lay people were also divided on the issue of parochial school education. Religious education, beginning in the home, took place in the first language of immigrant families who came from non-English-speaking countries, along with traditional, home-based religious celebrations. Thus many Catholic children began their doctrinal education in languages other than English. Some Catholics, particularly ethnic Germans, Slovaks, Polish, and French Canadians, sought to provide their children with schools that would transmit their language and culture along with religion and basic knowledge. In some of these ethnic parish communities, 70 to over 90 percent of children were in parochial schools by the 1890s.

Ethnic groups whose settlements were more scattered, particularly those living in rural areas, experienced greater difficulty in funding parish schools and in finding teachers qualified to staff them. A 1906 survey of 514 predominantly Mexican, Spanish-speaking parishes found that only six had parochial schools. In addition, recently arrived, poorly paid immigrants in large cities were often either financially unable to pay school tuition or to make contributions for parish schools, or simply were not incorporated into the larger Catholic culture in the U.S. at this time. A 1908 U.S. government survey found that only some 15 percent of Italian children in urban centers attended parochial schools.

Other ethnic and mixed parishes, such as those with predominantly English or Irish populations, did not view public schools to be as threatening with regard to cultural traditions and language. As a result they did not mobilize as rapidly to organize Catholic schools. In 1898, the Archdiocese of New York, led by parochial school advocate Archbishop Michael Corrigan, had only 50 percent of its parishes maintaining parochial schools, which served about one-third of the area's Catholic children. Overall, in 1900 only 37 percent of parishes in the U.S. supported parish schools, almost equal to the 38 percent that did so in 1883. By 1920, that level had dropped to 35 percent.

In general, large numbers of Catholics supported Catholic schools and greatly contributed to their development. As noted earlier, many Catholic parents highly valued Catholic school-based religious instruction for their children and sought an approach that respected their culture and, when possible, their language. For their part, Catholic religious orders found that the educational ministry fit well with their traditions, the needs of the institutional Church, and the exigencies of religious life. Women's orders based in the United States, such as the Sisters of Charity, and European orders, such as the School Sisters of Notre Dame and the Sisters of the Sacred Heart, grew significantly in the second part of the nineteenth century. Many women's orders were founded specifically to staff Catholic schools. In 1850, there were only 1,344 women religious in the United States, compared to 1,109 priests. By 1900, there were 40,340 women religious in the United States, compared to 11,636 priests. Their efforts to prepare teachers, combined with their availability at very low expenses, reduced the cost of Catholic schooling significantly and made opening schools a reality for parishes and missions that otherwise would not have been able to afford them. Men's religious orders, such as the Society of Jesus, the Christian Brothers, and the Congregation of the Holy Cross, also helped to promote Catholic education. Members of religious orders also opened mission schools for Native Americans and conducted work in

African American communities, many of which were otherwise neglected at the time.

Xenophobic non-Catholics saw Catholic schools as a plot to undermine national unity. Some Catholics had feared that Catholic schools would either ghettoize Catholics from U.S. society at large or foment divisions within the Church along ethnic and linguistic lines. However, Catholic schools actually served a transformative function, helping recently arrived immigrants and their children gain the skills necessary to advance in U.S. society (the use of English, even in Catholic schools that served those of a single ethnic origin, spread relatively rapidly), while at the same time supporting the family's religious values and ethnic identities, and fostering a sense of community support and respect for learning.

Standardization

As the Catholic educational system expanded, concerns arose from within and outside the Church regarding educational standards. At the turn of the century, overcrowding and insufficient funding were common complaints in both Catholic and public schools. The public schools sought to improve their quality by improving teacher training, enforcing attendance, and systematizing the curricula and rules of the schools. Catholic schools also addressed these concerns, and followed the same trends. At times, the education of Catholic school teachers, especially women religious, had been given low priority. However, the establishment of Catholic high schools and colleges, including academies and colleges for women, helped to encourage improvement of the educational training of members of religious orders as well as lay teachers in parochial schools.

Significant differences in curricula (for example, American history based on the contributions of different ethnic groups) also raised concern on diocesan as well as public school boards. The barriers of language and culture were hard to surmount, as ethnic groups and local pastors were suspicious of plans to centralize the direction of Catholic education. The promotion of the accreditation of Catholic schools and colleges and their growing similarities with the structure of public and non-Catholic schools gradually overrode these concerns, bringing most Catholic schools on par with general standards in elementary, high school, and university education by the 1920s. These broader trends were also promoted by mandates from the Vatican, such as the centralizing effects of the proclamation of papal infallibility at the First Vatican Council in 1870, the revival of Scholastic philosophy in the late nineteenth and early twentieth centuries to engage with liberal and modernist thought, and the approval of a conservative educational program in the 1929 encyclical *Divini Illius Magistri* (On the Christian Education of Youth).

After more than a century of legal debates, the U.S. Supreme Court ruled in favor of the existence of private schools in 1925, finding an Oregon state law mandating attendance at public schools to be unconstitutional (*Pierce v. Society of Sisters*). While private schools were made to comply with state-approved academic curricula, periods of attendance, and standards of accreditation, they were and are free to develop their own special curricula. By the middle of the twentieth century, Catholic schools had developed into an extensive system ranging from early childhood education to advanced university training, comparable in standards to the public school educational system, while at the same time being self-assured in its mission to socialize and educate Catholic youth in their faith.

Continuity and Change

Catholic elementary and high school enrollments were at their peak in the 1960s: 12 percent of all elementary and secondary students in the United States, roughly 5.5 million students, were enrolled in over 13,000 Catholic schools in 1965. During this same period, the great success of Catholic education led to considerable questioning. Writers such as Mary Perkins Ryan asked *Are Parochial Schools the Answer?* (1964), questioning the continued need for Catholic schooling two generations after the end of large-scale European immigration and the decline of virulent anti-Catholicism. As in virtually all other areas of the Church, the Second Vatican Council heralded significant changes for Catholic education in the United States. Pope John XXIII's *aggiornamento* included scrutiny of the educational role of the Church, and a lifting of Church-promoted restrictions on pedagogy and curricular standards.

However, far from spelling the end of Catholic education, the Council's 1965 declaration *Gravissimum Educationis* (On Christian Education) called for a renewal of the mission of Catholic educational institutions. The school environment was to be "enlivened by the spirit of freedom and charity" and should act as the "leaven of the human community." In 1972, the bishops of the United States released *To Teach as Jesus Did*, a document calling for active, publicly engaged Catholic schools. Catholic schools were to teach principles of the Gospel in light of its message of hope, encourage the real building of community as opposed to its being taught as an intellectual concept, and then to encourage service based on membership in the larger community. *Brothers and Sisters to Us* (1979) emphasized Catholic schools' ministry to disadvantaged populations. These and subsequent documents affirmed what many Catholic schools and the religious communities that served them had been doing for decades, if not longer. Resisting the initial temptation to let school enrollments swell, U.S. bishops and other Catholic leaders refused to let Catholic schools become a haven for "white flight" from city centers and newly integrated public schools. Parishes and religious orders have kept open Catholic schools that provide educational opportunities for inner-city children even as demographic changes have resulted in a student body no longer solely or even primarily Catholic. Since the 1960s, non-Catholic enrollment in Catholic schools has increased markedly.

Recently, many Catholic schools have suffered from financial crises. The Catholic school system had been based in great part on the service of women and men religious who dedicated themselves to educational missions despite enormous self-sacrifice. Some religious, following the Vatican II mandate to review the constitutions of their congregations, chose to prioritize areas of social service other than education. Many members accordingly left their schools. Between 1964 and 1984, 40 percent of Catholic high schools and 27 percent of Catholic elementary schools closed. In 1967, religious sisters, brothers, and priests had made up 58 percent of the teachers in Catholic elementary and secondary schools. By 1983, they comprised only 24 percent of the teachers, and in 1990, less than 15 percent. Today, that figure is 7 percent.

As a result, Catholic schooling, from the elementary to the university level, has had to absorb an enormous increase in salary expenses as schools changed to virtually all lay staffs. Dioceses and parishes that have developed a diversity of programs and struggle to distribute resources fairly have less money to allocate to schools. This, along with increasing demands for better, high-technology facilities, has prompted dramatic tuition increases, thus putting at risk the principle that students from all socioeconomic strata should be able to attend Catholic schools.

This financial problem has been exacerbated by falling numbers of enrollments as well. The numbers of Catholic children attending Catholic schools began to drop in the 1960s, due to both a decline in the birth rate and the Vatican II-era debate regarding the need to educate Catholic children in parochial schools. In 1990, Catholic schools enrolled approximately 5.5 million students, or 5.4 percent of the U.S. school-age population, in about 9,000 schools.[2] In 1998, that percentage was about the same: 2.7 million students, or 5.5 percent of the U.S. school-age population, were enrolled in 6,925 Catholic elementary and high schools. For all these changes, Catholic schools remain vital Catholic cultural institutions that transmit and reflect Catholic values and teaching to the next generation.

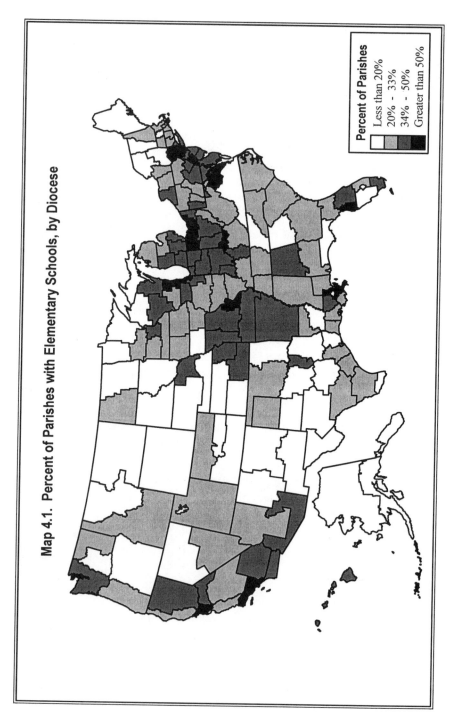

Map 4.1. Percent of Parishes with Elementary Schools, by Diocese

Percent of Parishes
Less than 20%
20% - 33%
34% - 50%
Greater than 50%

Catholic School-age Children

Perhaps the most accurate way to estimate the population of Catholic school-age children, and therefore the percent enrolled in Catholic schools or participating in parish religion education programs, is from baptismal records. Table 4.1 compares the numbers of Catholic school-age children in 1950 and 1998, the most recent year for which data are available.[3] It makes no estimates of deaths or conversions, and assumes that all infant baptisms were close to the time of birth.

Table 4.1. Estimated School-age Catholics

Estimated Age	Grade in School	1950 Birth Year	1950 School-age Children	1998 Birth Year	1998 School-age Children
1		1949	943,433	1998	970,249
2		1948	937,208	1997	1,001,049
3		1947	907,294	1996	1,003,611
4	Pre-K	1946	738,314	1995	981,444
5	Pre-K	1945	705,557	1994	1,019,442
	Total pre-school		1,443,871		2,000,886
6	Kindergarten	1944	710,648	1993	992,970
7	First	1943	722,434	1992	1,009,561
8	Second	1942	700,446	1991	1,026,152
9	Third	1941	678,457	1990	1,037,213
10	Fourth	1940	656,468	1989	991,758
11	Fifth	1939	634,479	1988	946,303
12	Sixth	1938	612,490	1987	937,947
13	Seventh	1937	590,501	1986	941,898
14	Eighth	1936	568,512	1985	953,323
	Total K-8		5,874,435		8,837,125
15	Ninth	1935	546,523	1984	947,668
16	Tenth	1934	524,534	1983	975,017
17	Eleventh	1933	502,545	1982	965,049
18	Twelfth	1932	480,556	1981	982,586
	Total 9-12		2,054,158		3,870,320
	Grand Total pre-K-12		9,372,464		14,708,331

Elementary Schools

In 1950, there were 8,128 parish elementary schools, or approximately one for every two of the 15,104 parishes in the U.S. In some dioceses, the ratio of parishes with schools was as high as one to one. Table 4.2 shows the number of parish and private Catholic elementary schools and their approximate enrollment.[4]

Table 4.2. Catholic Elementary Schools and Students		
	1950	1998
Parish Schools	8,128	6,649
Private Schools	529	276
Total Schools	8,657	6,925
Total Parishes	15,104	19,181
Percent of Parishes with Schools	54%	35%
Average Enrollment per School	305	290
Total K-8 Enrollment	2,644,184	2,009,065
Estimated Proportion Catholic	99%	87%
Catholic K-8 Enrollments	2,617,742	1,747,887
Total Catholic K-8 Children	5,874,435	8,837,125
Percent Catholic Children Enrolled in Catholic Schools	45%	20%

Thus, while the number of Catholic parishes has increased by more than a quarter since 1950, the number of parishes with Catholic schools decreased by about a fifth, from 54 percent to 35 percent of all Catholic parishes, declining from their mid-century peak to turn of the century levels. Catholic school enrollments declined by a third, though there are more Catholic school children of elementary school-age than ever.

In 1950, about 45 percent of all Catholic children were enrolled in parochial elementary schools. In 1998, only some 20 percent of all baptized Catholic school-age children attended parish schools.

High Schools

In the nineteenth century, Catholic high schools or academies were often combined with college or university education (following the European, Jesuit-developed system), or functioned as preparatory training for the advanced study required for entering men's religious orders. Toward the turn of the twentieth century, however, the growing need for broader access to education above the elementary level prompted the development of independent Catholic high schools, which soon modified their curricula to parallel the general U.S. pattern of a four-year course of study. Because they were more expensive to operate than elementary schools, fewer parishes could sponsor their own high schools. Bishops encouraged parishes to establish central, multi-parish high schools. Religious orders also opened high schools for Catholic young men and women. By the mid-twentieth century, the Jesuits and Christian Brothers ran many high schools for boys, and numerous women's religious orders operated high schools and academies for girls.

Catholic high schools have been affected as well by the drop in birth rate and enrollments, loss of teachers from religious orders, rising expenses, and changes in the priority given to Catholic education. However, their reputation for providing high-quality education in nurturing environments, particularly those in inner-city neighborhoods, has helped to sustain the Catholic high school as a vital institution. There are half as many parish or diocesan high schools today as in 1950, but enrollments today are more than 600,000.[5] However, due to growth in the Catholic population, enrollment as a proportion of Catholic youth is nonetheless lower. In 1950, one in four Catholic children ages 15-18 was enrolled in Catholic high schools. In 1998, that ratio was one in seven.

Table 4.3. High Schools and Students		
	1950	**1998**
Diocesan or Parish Schools	1,581	732
Private Schools	789	513
Total Schools	2,370	1,245
Average Enrollments Per School	222	505
Total 9-12 Enrollment	525,114	628,574
Proportion Catholic	99%	87%
Catholic 9-12 Enrollments	519,863	546,859
Total Catholic 9-12 Children	2,054,158	3,870,320

TEACHERS IN CATHOLIC SCHOOLS

In 1950, teachers in Catholic elementary and high schools numbered 110,272, more than three-quarters of whom were women religious. At the time, about 55 percent of all sisters, or 83,583, taught in Catholic schools. About 45 percent of all religious brothers, or 3,450, were school teachers. Just under one in five priests, or 7,785, also taught in Catholic schools. Only 14 percent of all teachers in Catholic elementary and high schools were lay teachers. Table 4.4 compares 1950 and 1998 on these numbers.

Table 4.4. Teachers in Catholic Elementary and High Schools

| | 1950 | | 1998 | |
	Number	Percent	Number	Percent
Sisters	83,583	76%	9,200	6%
Priests	7,785	7	1,900	1
Scholastics	416	<1	42	<1
Brothers	3,450	3	1,114	<1
Lay Teachers	15,038	14	149,710	93
Total	110,272	100	161,966	100

Current figures on teachers in Catholic elementary and high schools reflect a dramatic change.[6] Figure 4.1 shows the distribution of teachers in

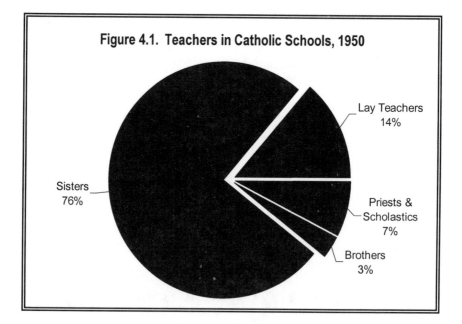

Figure 4.1. Teachers in Catholic Schools, 1950

Lay Teachers
14%

Sisters
76%

Priests &
Scholastics
7%

Brothers
3%

Catholic schools in 1950, more than three-quarters of whom were religious sisters. But by 1998, the most recent year for which figures are available, over 90 percent of teachers in Catholic schools were lay persons, as can be seen in Figure 4.2. The reasons for this transformation are complicated, but one result is that Catholic schools today pay more for teachers and are more likely to draw their administrative staff from laity, as well.

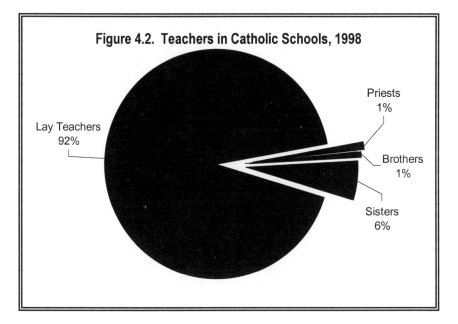

Figure 4.2. Teachers in Catholic Schools, 1998

Priests 1%

Lay Teachers 92%

Brothers 1%

Sisters 6%

PARISH-BASED RELIGIOUS EDUCATION PROGRAMS

Parish-based religious education programs are also sometimes known as "CCD Programs," by virtue of their association with the Confraternity of Christian Doctrine (CCD). In his 1905 encyclical *Acerbo Nimis* (On Teaching Christian Doctrine), Pope Pius X mandated that CCDs be organized in all countries to address the concern that the growing number of Catholics enrolled in public, secular educational programs rather than in Catholic schools would remain ignorant of Catholic doctrine. The CCD in this country was largely built up as part of the efforts of clergy and laity in the early twentieth century to expand the role and scope of Catholic social services. The CCD interpreted the goal to "foster and promote the teaching of Christ as handed down by the Roman Catholic Church" to include the organization of separate religious education programs for children and adults, as well as reviewing the educational materials to be used by them. Today, the successor of the original CCD effort is one of the largest and most extensive national apostolates supervised by the United States Catholic Conference.[7] These programs are used to transmit Catholic teachings to Catholic school-age children not attending Catholic schools, as well as to prepare them for participation in the sacraments of Reconciliation, First Eucharist, and Confirmation.

In 1950, 1,763,121 Catholic children attending public schools were receiving religious instruction outside of their public school hours. Pope

Pius X's original mandate was to parish priests, instructing them to hold classes on Sundays for the Catholic children in their care. However, this ministry was gradually delegated to vowed religious and lay people, the latter of whom now dominate the ranks of religious education teachers. Many parish programs are conducted on Sundays, often integrated with Sunday Masses, but in other parishes, this instruction takes place as part of released-time agreements with the local school boards or departments of education. At the request of their parents, Catholic public school children are permitted to leave during school hours to attend religious instruction classes held off public school premises, usually at parochial schools or in church halls. Today, some 7,627,629 Catholic children attending public schools receive religious education. This is more than a four-fold increase in reported enrollments for 1950.

Even more impressive, however, is the shift in the percent of Catholic school-age children who do *not* attend Catholic schools and instead attend these programs, shown in the enrollment figures in Table 4.5. In 1950, parish-based religious education enrolled about 1.8 million of a total of

Table 4.5. Children in Parish-based Religious Education		
	1950	**1998**
Total School-Age Catholic Children	9,372,464	14,708,331
Catholic children in Catholic schools	3,137,605	2,294,746
Percent of Catholic children in Catholic Schools	33%	16%
Potential Catholic School-age Children not Enrolled in Catholic Schools	4,752,648	12,413,585
Children Enrolled in Parish-based Religious Education	1,763,121	7,627,629
As a Percent of all Catholic School-age Children	19%	52%
As a Percent of all Catholic School-age Children not enrolled in Catholic Schools	37%	61%
Percent of all Catholic School-age Children in some form of Catholic education program	52%	67%

4.8 million Catholic school-age children who were not in Catholic schools. In the most recent figures available, about 7.6 million of 12 million

Catholic school-age children not in Catholic schools were enrolled in these programs. In other words, about 37 percent of Catholic children not in Catholic schools were in parish religious education in 1950; the figure today is closer to 61 percent. As a result of this much greater extent of parish religious education programs, the overall percentage of Catholic school-age children covered by some form of Catholic education, whether Catholic schools or parish programs, has increased from about 52 percent to about 67 percent over the past half century.

Many earlier CCD programs were not much different than religion classes in Catholic schools in that they were based wholesale on the same texts and techniques used for a daily school environment. While the pedagogy of these programs has become more attuned to the different patterns and needs of its students, there are still limits to what can be conveyed in weekly versus daily meetings. However, researchers have found that Catholics in the U.S. who attended extracurricular, parish-based religious education programs do not report noticeably less favorable responses with regard to agreement with teachings of the Catholic Church; nor do they score noticeably worse on survey questions of basic recollection of Church doctrine and teachings.[8] Table 4.6 compares results of those who attended Catholic schools to those who attended CCD, with corresponding results for their children, from CARA's Catholic Poll 2000.

Table 4.6. Influence of Catholic Education on Aspects of Being Catholic

Percent of Catholics who identify each as "Very Important"

	Respondent		Respondent's Children	
	Attended Catholic School	Attended CCD	Attended Catholic School	Attended CCD
Helping Those in Need	78%	78%	79%	80%
Passing on Faith	67	68	81	62
Eucharist	65	61	79	58
Catholic Faith	58	48	75	48
Attending Mass	49	52	66	47
Following Church	49	47	57	43
Learning Catholic Teaching	43	44	52	39
Devotions	38	42	50	38

Table 4.7. Influence of Catholic Education on Satisfaction				
Percent of Catholics who say they are "Very Satisfied"				
	Respondent		Respondent's Children	
	Attended Catholic School	Attended CCD	Attended Catholic School	Attended CCD
Church	37%	38%	50%	33%
Leadership	30	31	36	30

One important concern revealed in the 1995 study cited above was an underlying dissatisfaction with CCD programs, particularly those of the 1970s and 1980s. Former participants sometimes feel that the education they had been given was "watered down," or that more was taught about "being nice to each other" than about the history or teachings of the Catholic Church. In any case, the trans-mission of the traditions of the Church to the next generations of Catholics will depend more and more on these programs.

COMPARATIVE DEMOGRAPHICS
OF CATHOLIC EDUCATION

There does, however, seem to be a level of correlation between the participation of Catholics in some form of Catholic education, whether full or part time, and the participation of their children in some form of Catholic educational program. As data from the CARA Catholic Poll 2000

Table 4.8. Catholic Education				
	Respondent		Respondent's Children	
	Attended Catholic School	Attended CCD	Attended Catholic School	Attended CCD
World War II Generation	47%	45%	71%	71%
Silent Generation	58	59	63	70
Vatican II Generation	57	65	41	65
Young Adult Generation	43	66	18	36

show in Table 4.8, the World War II generation of Catholics report rather low levels of their own attendance in Catholic educational programs, but their high rate of sending their children to Catholic schools and religious education programs may be related to periods of expansion in the Catholic school system and to experiences of post-war prosperity. More than half of the Silent Generation and Vatican II Generation report having attended Catholic schools and Catholic religious education programs, but the Young Adult Generation is much less likely to have attended Catholic school and more likely to have attended religious education. This youngest adult generation of Catholics also reports the lowest levels of participation in Catholic education for their children. Fewer than one in five say their children attend a Catholic school, and just over a third say their children attend Catholic religious education.

COLLEGES AND UNIVERSITIES

Georgetown University, founded in 1789, was the first Catholic college in the United States. Many others followed, particularly in the late nineteenth century, as the Catholic population grew and the challenge to meet the educational needs of a growing Catholic middle class increased. A good number of smaller Catholic colleges and universities began as teaching colleges and nursing training schools for religious women that later expanded their enrollment to laywomen, or as schools opened specifically to educate women who found admission closed to them at both Catholic and non-Catholic institutes of higher learning.

The number of Catholic colleges and universities today is almost identical to 50 years ago, but the number of students at those colleges and universities has tripled.

Table 4.9. Catholic College and University Enrollments		
	1950	**1998**
Catholic Colleges and Universities	234	233
Average Enrollment per School	986	2,904
Total Enrollments	230,774	676,646

The percent of students who are themselves Catholic varies from school to school, usually from 60 to 80 percent. This is largely a function of the environment in which the school finds itself and the students it was designed to serve according to its mission or that of the religious institute that founded it.

The map shows the location of Catholic colleges and universities that are affiliated with the Association of Catholic Colleges and Universities (ACCU). Table 4.10 shows enrollments and founding dates of 30 largest.

Table 4.10. Catholic Colleges and Universities with the Highest Student Enrollments in 1999

Name	Sponsor	Founded	1999 Enrollment
DePaul University	Vincentians	1898	19,511
St. John's University (NY)	Vincentians	1870	18,478
Boston College	Jesuits	1863	14,652
Fordham University	Jesuits	1841	13,551
Loyola University Chicago	Jesuits	1870	13,359
Georgetown University	Jesuits	1789	12,498
Regis University	Jesuits	1877	12,000
St. Louis University	Jesuits	1818	11,069
University of St. Thomas (MN)	Archdiocesan	1885	10,929
Marquette University	Jesuits	1881	10,780
University of Dayton	Marianists	1850	10,223
Notre Dame University	Holy Cross	1842	10,301
Seton Hall University	Archdiocesan	1856	10,096
Villanova University	Augustinians	1842	9,951
Duquesne University	Holy Ghost	1878	9,742
Saint Leo University	Benedictines	1889	8,020
Barry University	Dominicans	1940	7,909
Santa Clara University	Jesuits	1851	7,707
University of San Francisco	Jesuits	1855	7,803
Saint Joseph's University	Jesuits	1851	6,800
College of New Rochelle	Ursulines	1904	6,500
Creighton University	Jesuits	1878	6,325
University of Detroit-Mercy*	Jesuits/ Mercy Sisters	1877	6,300
Loyola College (MD)	Jesuits	1852	6,263
University of San Diego	Diocesan	1949	6,100
Sacred Heart University	Diocesan	1963	6,000
Seattle University	Jesuits	1891	5,990
The Catholic University of America	U.S. Bishops	1887	5,600
Iona College	Christian Brothers	1940	5,600
Fairfield University	Jesuits	1942	5,208

* The University of Detroit merged with Mercy College of Detroit (founded by the Sisters of Mercy in 1941) in 1990.

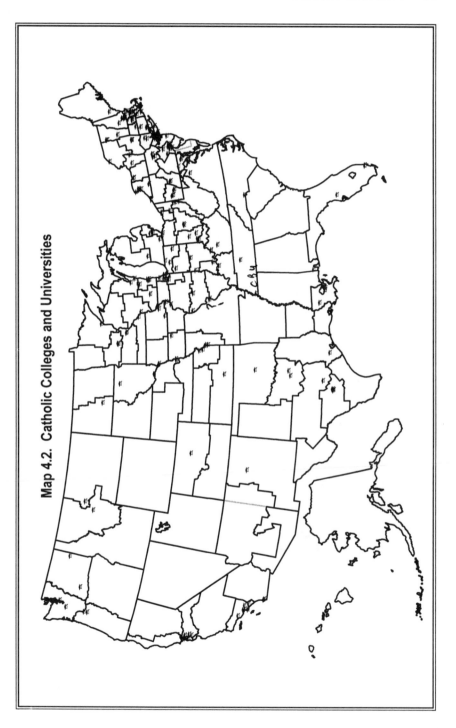

Map 4.2. Catholic Colleges and Universities

As discussed above, in the early twentieth century Catholic higher education was modified to fit the U.S. pattern of four years of high school and four years of undergraduate education. Catholic colleges and universities as separate entities shared in the general expansion of university education in America, especially after the Second World War, when the G.I. Bill enabled many more Americans to enroll in higher education.   In 1916, there were 8,304 full-time students enrolled in Catholic colleges; in 1950, there were 112,765. The number of Catholic women's colleges also increased dramatically in the same period: in 1906, there were 19, but by 1950 their number had increased to 116 out of 175 Catholic higher education institutions.

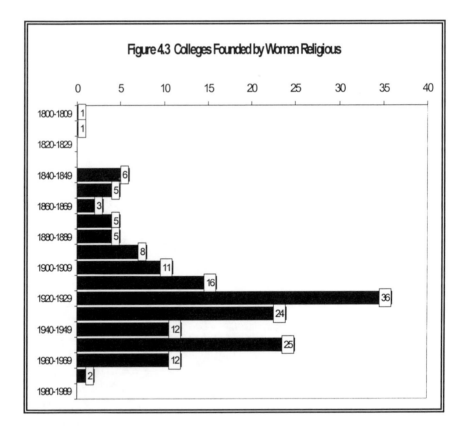

Figure 4.3 Colleges Founded by Women Religious

In the 1930s, Catholic intellectuals such as novelist Flannery O'Connor and sociologist Thomas O'Dea pointed out that the Catholic university system's strong emphasis on devotional Catholicism and its bias toward a canon based on translated European works and works of British origin might well be holding Catholic universities back from taking a place at the forefront of U.S. higher education. Addressing this issue, some universities sought to expand their research capacities and graduate programs, which before that time had been largely limited to the Catholic University of America. Two successive presidents of Notre Dame University, John J. Cavanaugh, CSC, and Theodore M. Hesburgh, CSC, devoted considerable time and energy to altering the reputation of their institution from representing excellence on the football field to excellence in advanced education and research. In general, however, the Jesuits had come to dominate the field of higher education for Catholics by the mid-twentieth century, and then sought to develop graduate programs within their colleges and universities as well. As a result, universities such as Boston College, Fordham, Georgetown, Holy Cross, and St. Louis strengthened their national standing. Many more Catholic colleges continue to provide undergraduate-level education for a diverse range of students. Several of these are ranked among the top 50 U.S. colleges and universities.[9]

CATHOLIC IDENTITY

Given the structural imperatives of academia, institutional development, government subsidies, and other debates regarding dependence on or independence from Church institutions such as religious orders, dioceses, and parishes, the issue of Catholic identity is particularly complex for Catholic universities. The Second Vatican Council's encouragement of openness intensified trends to diversify curricula and faculty at U.S. Catholic colleges and universities. These institutions already had begun to hire faculty based on academic credentials rather than religious commitment, as part of the pursuit of high standards of academic excellence. During the late 1960s and 1970s, in response to hiring demands as the number of faculty from religious orders declined and the number of students increased, large numbers of faculty with considerably less Catholic background or commitment came into these institutions. During that same period, many Catholic colleges and universities placed themselves under the supervision of lay boards of trustees, rather than religious orders, as part of an effort to bring them into step with modern practices of academe and business administration. As leadership, faculty, and practices became less formally Catholic, debates arose as to what it meant to be a "Catholic" university or college.

Concerned with these shifts, Catholics sought to address the question of Catholic identity in higher education. The International Federation of Catholic Universities (ICFU) called for dialogue on the future of Catholic higher education in 1965. The Association of Catholic Colleges and Universities, representing Catholic college and university presidents, met in Land O'Lakes, Wisconsin, and reached a consensus on the distinctive character of the Catholic university in contemporary times. The 1967 *Land O'Lakes Statement on the Nature of the Contemporary University* stressed academic freedom and institutional autonomy, while at the same time it promoted a commitment to preserve Catholicism as a visible presence in college and university life. This document, along with responses from other countries, was combined in *The Catholic University in the Modern World*, drawn up after a 1972 meeting of the ICFU in Rome. It helped to guide Catholic higher education until 1990, when it was supplanted by the papal encyclical *Ex Corde Ecclesiae* (On Catholic Universities). After much debate and discussion, the bishops of the U.S. approved a plan to implement the encyclical in November 1999.

Even before the encyclical, Catholic colleges and universities worldwide were bound to follow the provision of the Code of Canon Law that states that their theologians must have approval to teach Catholic theology (c.812). Essentially, *Ex Corde Ecclesiae* addresses the concern that the individualist pull towards academic freedom might undermine the sense of community and of Catholic identity in colleges and universities associated with the Church. It calls for tighter links between Church institutions and Catholic colleges and universities as a way of assuring continued Catholic identity and the university. On the other hand, *Ex Corde Ecclesiae* and the bishops' document implementing it in the United States presented this concern in a rich philosophical context that respects cultural issues in a broader community, emphasizes the sense of community that colleges and universities can nurture, and affirms that Catholic colleges and universities should provide such an atmosphere for the diverse communities in which they are situated. Although the questions raised by academic debate and Vatican decree are difficult to resolve, they have in no way dimmed the renewed enthusiasm of many Catholic colleges and universities to continue their educational missions within a context informed by their Catholic faith and intellectual tradition.

As shown in Table 4.9, Catholic college and university enrollment has grown at a healthy rate. Catholic student enrollment also remains relatively high. One difficulty common to all Catholic institutions of education is rising tuition costs; an unfortunate consequence of recent trends, as well as inflation, has been the pressure to have tuition charges reflect market forces. Some prestigious Catholic universities now charge tuition equivalent to that of Ivy League schools. In addition, smaller, less-competitive schools often must charge fees greater than $10,000 per year to meet expenses. This makes it somewhat more difficult for Catholic higher educational institutions to fulfill their original mission to provide a quality, Catholic education for the diverse population of Catholics in the United States. Today, those in the working and middle classes, for whom many of these institutions were founded, cannot afford to attend Catholic colleges or universities without financial assistance.[10]

A growing number of Catholic college-level students attend non-Catholic institutions of higher education; it is estimated that two out of every three Catholics attending college is at a non-Catholic university. Many students, with the support of clergy and lay ministers, have promoted the growth of Catholic student societies and ministries. One of the first of these was the Newman Movement, founded at the University of Wisconsin in 1883 "to support the pastoral care and religious education in non-Catholic colleges and universities." In the 1960s, priests and vowed religious began to prioritize this ministry, and established Catholic campus ministries at many secular campuses. At present, the Catholic Campus Ministry Association estimates that over 3,000 college and university campuses have a Catholic campus ministry. Of these, only about 14 percent are Catholic higher education institutions; 30 percent are at private, non-Catholic institutions; 53 percent are at public, two- and four-year institutions; and three percent at other institutions of higher education.[11]

CONCLUSION

At the beginning of the twenty-first century, a number of broad shifts in the strength and structure of Catholic education that have taken place are clear. Catholic school leadership and personnel are for the most part no longer men and women religious. At the same time, many schools founded by religious communities have passed from religious communities' direct ownership to that of self-perpetuating boards of directors comprised of laity and religious.

Catholic parishes are now more likely not to have an elementary school than to have one, and Catholics are more likely to receive their religious education in a parish-based program than a parochial or private Catholic school environment. Today, the component of Catholic education that has the broadest reach is that of parish-based catechesis.

Catholic schools are more likely than ever to have non-Catholics enrolled in their programs, which generally have reputations for being communities of learning, distinguished for academic quality.

Catholic education has undergone considerable growth and transformation over the past century. Schools originally created and maintained by vowed religious are now almost entirely in the hands of lay professionals. The student populations at Catholic schools have become more diverse, a result of the opening of Catholic charitable services and institutions to the community at large, and a desire on the part of Catholics to engage with the broader academic community and with society. The "market share" of Catholic schools in terms of the percent of all Catholic children and youth who attend them has declined, but the overall numbers and percentage of Catholic school-age children served by some form of Catholic education or ministry has increased. It may be that the Church's turn to more parish-based catechetical programs, combined with new and creative cooperative relationships in education and funding with public and private institutions, will become a hallmark of the Church's educational mission in the United States.

Enrollment in Catholic elementary schools has increased somewhat, but that increase is eclipsed by the increase in the number of Catholic children registered in religious education programs outside of school hours. However, enrollments in high schools, colleges and universities are actually higher, both in individual schools and overall, now than they were at mid-century. The number of Catholic educational institutions is smaller, as some universities and schools have cut or minimized their religious affiliations, and religious orders and parishes no longer emphasize educational institutions in the same manner.

In response to the difficulties in maintaining and funding parish schools, parishes increasingly act together to establish central schools in order to pool resources and raise student enrollment, as has already occurred with Catholic regional high schools. Also, some colleges and universities have consolidated in order to be able to maintain themselves financially and compete in the modern educational system. Existing schools have consolidated into larger or regional units. From the elementary through the university level, some formerly single-sex schools have become coeducational, either by opening their enrollment to both males and females or by merging with another institution to combine enrollment.

Catholic schools, from elementary to universities, are addressing their need to approach the government and private sector for support while continuing to balance their commitment to the Catholic faith with the goal to provide opportunities for the pursuit of knowledge to all members of their institutions, Catholic and non-Catholic alike.

CHAPTER 5

Social Service Institutions and Agencies

CHANGE AND CONTINUITY

In the mid-nineteenth century, the Catholic population of the United States began to grow significantly due to incoming streams of European immigrants. Many settled in cities in the Northeast and Midwest, and initially made up a large part of the working class. Social reformers of that time found that many of the urban poor as well as those in orphanages, prisons, and other correctional or social service institutions were Catholic. While Nativist extremists rejected Catholic immigrants as a lost cause, other social reformers looked upon Catholicism as a kind of social dysfunction that could be cured by placement in middle-class, Protestant homes and by eventual conversion.

Catholics were motivated to action by this situation and by the growing reform movements of the post Civil War United States in areas such as education, labor reform, child welfare, and temperance, which, if not explicitly secular, often had Protestant overtones. In response, Catholics began to create and support an extensive network of charitable institutions. As a result, charitable work, particularly involving children and health care, became a cornerstone of Catholic life in the United States.

Over the past 150 years, Catholic charitable work has grown dramatically in scope and importance. What started as local efforts undertaken by religious orders or parish, ethnic, and charitable associations has become one of the largest social service networks in the United States.

Much of this growth is in great part due to the dedication and talent of the women religious and their collaborators who created, led, and staffed Catholic charitable institutions throughout the nineteenth and twentieth centuries.   The Catholic Church in the United States successfully transcended parochial and ethnic divisions to establish norms, standards, and a degree of centralized coordination in its charitable works. At the same time, its new organizational structure preserved sufficient autonomy at diocesan, parish, and institutional levels to enable Catholic health care and other charitable efforts to adapt to changes over time and provide relevant services to meet local needs.

This chapter examines the evolution and current status of three important kinds of charitable work provided under Catholic auspices: health care, social services, and overseas service. In all three areas, the pattern has been a shift from individuals and associations generously dedicating themselves to service, as in the case of women religious running a hospital, to the centralization of these works into larger, more professionalized institutions and larger networks.

For the most part, congregations of religious no longer own or run hospitals as they once did. Instead, these institutions are supervised by professional boards of management, in conjunction with boards of trustees, under the auspices of a religious order, diocese, or other Catholic agency. Thus, many Catholic hospitals have become parts of regionally based systems, often beyond a diocesan level of coordination.

Outside of hospitals, in response to contemporary patterns of health care, Catholic health maintenance organizations and other new providers and services have been formed to respond to a new social and legal environment. While more specialized than earlier enterprises, they retain the spirit of Catholic charity by providing for the common good and the dignity of all human life.

As in the case of health care, other Catholic social service organizations have also been shaped by the forces of specialization, professionalization, and centralization. Other Catholic charitable efforts that are not focused on direct services themselves, such as the Catholic Campaign for Human Development, focus on advancing Catholic social teaching, and function as a funding organization rather than a direct service provider.

Internationally, Catholic Relief Services, an institution that developed out of lay Catholic charitable mobilization for soldiers, medical workers and refugees during World War II, has expanded in its overseas service and professional apparatus during a time when religious communities have reduced the number of members in missions overseas. This organization continues its mission by making a real difference in the quality of life of millions of people across Africa, Asia, Eastern Europe, and Latin America.

CATHOLIC HEALTH CARE INSTITUTIONS

Catholic Hospitals and Medical Care

The earliest and most visible elements of Catholic charitable institutions in the United States were Catholic hospitals and orphanages, founded in great part by women's religious orders. During the early nineteenth century, nursing was neither considered a respectable profession for single women nor one for which women were particularly suited, but the combination of dedication of women religious to nursing as a ministry, their willingness to work in harsh conditions and for subsistence pay, and their vows of poverty, chastity, and obedience, served to change the perspective of doctors and other critics.

The Ursulines came to New Orleans in 1727 with the intent to minister to the sick. By 1820, women religious outnumbered the priests working in the United States, and their numbers steadily increased to form the majority of those working in Catholic health care.

The Daughters of Charity opened their first hospital in St. Louis in 1829, and soon established other hospitals throughout the country. Similarly, the Sisters of Mercy opened hospitals in Pittsburgh and Chicago in the 1840s, and many others across much of the U.S. in succeeding decades. The Sisters of Charity provided similar services, primarily in the Midwest, while the Sisters of Providence founded hospitals throughout the Northwest.

The roles of women religious increased exponentially during epidemics such as the outbreaks of cholera in urban centers in the 1830s, 1840s, and 1860s, including efforts during the Civil War. Among the religious orders that distinguished themselves for their services were the Sisters of Charity, the Daughters of Charity, the Sisters of Mercy, the Congregation of the Sisters of the Holy Cross, the Dominican Sisters, the Sisters of St. Joseph, the Sisters of Providence, the Franciscan Sisters of the Poor, the Sisters of Our Lady of Mount Carmel, and the Ursulines.

After the Civil War, several new dimensions were added to the provision of Catholic health care and charitable services. Men's orders, notably the Christian Brothers and the Alexian Brothers, a community of men dedicated to health care, increasingly ministered to populations that women's religious orders, restricted by provisions in their constitutions that limited their contact with men and boys, could not reach.

As the second and third generation of Catholic Americans entered the middle class, lay Catholics increasingly expressed an interest in partici-pating in Catholic charitable services as volunteers. Associations such as the St. Vincent de Paul Society, the Ladies of Charity, and numerous ladies' auxiliaries and sodalities, began to lend their support in fundraising and voluntary assistance at Catholic hospitals and residential institutions.

Catholic hospitals and health care services grew in response to the great need for services among Catholic immigrant communities, and also to the difficulties that Catholic priests experienced trying to gain admittance to minister at public and Protestant hospitals. By the 1880s, there were 119 Catholic hospitals. Between 1880 and 1906, 225 more were founded, and the following decade saw the founding of an additional 106.

The Catholic Health Association of the United States (CHA) was founded in 1915, initially as the Catholic Hospital Association, with the mission to "support and strengthen the Catholic health ministry in the United States," so that health care could be provided to all, particularly the poor and those least able to care for themselves. Women religious comprised the majority of the CHA's membership, although priests headed the organization until a change in the bylaws in 1965 permitted the office of president to be held by women religious.[1]

Table 5.1. Catholic Hospitals in 1950

Type	Number	Beds	Admissions
General Hospitals	759	98,828	4,745,581
Special Hospitals	108	8,368	53,347

In 1950, 867 Catholic hospitals took in over 4.8 million admissions.[2] Today, the number of annual admissions is over 73 million. Although the total number of Catholic hospitals has shrunk since 1950, a new category of related institutions, health care centers, has emerged. At present, over 1,000 Catholic hospitals and health care centers together serve nearly 80 million people. Catholic hospitals represent more than 10 percent of all non-federal hospitals in the U.S. today, and 15 percent of all hospital beds.[3]

Table 5.2. Catholic Hospitals in 1998

Type	Number	Admissions
Hospitals	583	73,686,802
Health Care Centers	527	5,198,284

Changes in the climate of health care provision in the United States have affected Catholic health care ministries. After the Second Vatican Council, many religious orders opted to provide health care in other settings or to engage in other ministries. Thus Catholic hospitals were soon affected by declining numbers of religious women on staff. The degree of Catholic commitment of lay staff often varies, as does the clientele of Catholic hospitals and health care services, which also has become much more diverse. The rising expenses of private hospital insurance and modern equipment has led to an increased reliance on funding and reimbursement for medical services from sources such as the federal government.

Some Catholic hospitals have been sold to private, for-profit corporations, or have been reorganized as independent institutions. Agreements have been established to maintain the Catholic identity of these institutions, but the extent of the religious imagery used, pastoral care provided, and internal ethical constraints (such as prohibitions on artificial birth control provision, abortion, assisted suicide, and fetal-tissue research) are still debated by institutions that employ and provide services to non-Catholics, and that receive funding from non-Catholic sources. In 1999, the CHA launched a three-year strategic plan to define Catholic identity, health policy and initiatives, standards of Church relations, and ministry for Catholic hospitals and health care organizations across the U.S.

Other Residential and Day Care Facilities

Residential care facilities operated under Catholic auspices include orphanages, homes for the aged, mentally ill, and other long-term care facilities, as well as day care and other short-term centers. The most recent available information suggests that there are more than 2,200 Catholic centers offering specialized services to almost 19.5 million persons.

Table 5.3. Residential Care Provided by Catholic Charitable Institutions

| | 1950 | | 1998 | |
Type	Number	Served	Number	Served
Protective Institution	153	13,052	NA*	NA
Home for Aged	261	13,775	940	331,439
Orphanage/Children Home	353	41,166	145	84,500
Day Care/Extended Day	NA	1,242	NA	131,945
Specialized Homes	NA	412	NA	202,404
Residence for Disabled	NA	335	NA	37,179

*NA=No data available

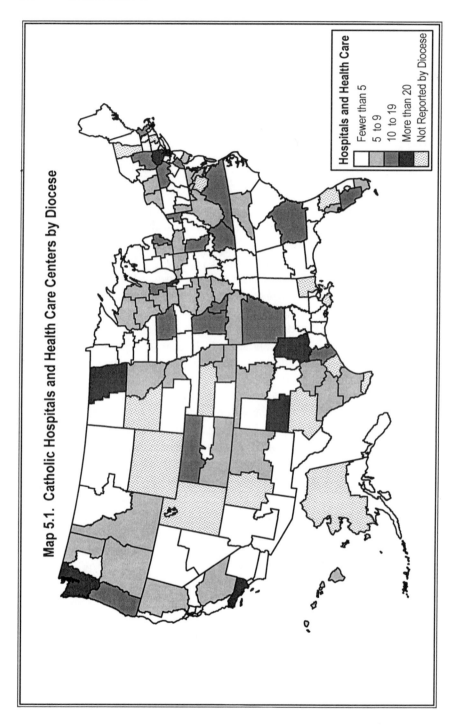

Map 5.1. Catholic Hospitals and Health Care Centers by Diocese

Hospitals and Health Care

Fewer than 5
5 to 9
10 to 19
More than 20
Not Reported by Diocese

CATHOLIC SOCIAL SERVICE INSTITUTIONS

From Catholic Charitable Efforts to Catholic Charities USA

The history of Catholic social services in the U.S. begins well before the founding of the present-day nation. Numerous missionaries and religious orders worked throughout the territories controlled by the French and Spanish, providing a wide variety of charitable services as well as evangelization. Elizabeth Seton founded the first orphanage and free school in Maryland in 1809, thereby setting the course for the next 150 years of the Catholic Church in the U.S. and for the religious order of sisters that she founded. The English colonial administration and the independent U.S. government had established some means to address poverty, through local administration, poor houses, indentured servitude, and the "placing out" of poor children and orphans. However, no significant national policies were designed to care for the poor until the 1930s, in response to the Great Depression. Until then, the provision of charity was sometimes undertaken by state-supported agencies, but more often fell to private and religiously affiliated associations, which at times worked in cooperation with local governments.

As the U.S. Catholic population grew in the nineteenth century, so did the scope of charitable services provided by the Church. Religious orders founded hospitals, hospices, orphanages, and schools, aided by dioceses and lay benefactors. They were also instrumental in the establishment of Catholic home missions to minister to populations of European immigrants, African Americans, and Asian Americans, as well as the Hispanic and Native American populations absorbed into the country after the conquests of their lands. Lay associations, organized along parish or ethnic lines, and local chapters of Catholic lay groups such as the St. Vincent de Paul Society (established in the U.S. in 1845), the Ladies of Charity, and individual sodalities and confraternities founded community organizations to provide emergency shelter, child care, work placement, and other forms of mutual aid. Most existed only at the local level, supervised in varying degrees by their diocesan bishops.

Some Church leaders, fearing anti-Catholic attacks on the Church, encouraged Catholic charitable organizations to avoid large-scale organization. In some cases, individual bishops worked to consolidate control over the raising and allocation of funds, and the distribution of charitable services provided in their diocese. At the same time, many women religious and other leaders of local Catholic charitable organizations resisted attempts to centralize, fearing a loss of control over their endeavors and fundraising.

The Civil War created needs that exceeded neighborhood and parish boundaries, as Catholic soldiers and non-combatants traveled great distances as part of their engagement with the conflict, and prompted some of the first more broadly based Catholic charitable networks. For the most part, however, there was little interaction among local groups, and even less organization on the diocesan or national level. With the advent of new social and psychological theories at the beginning of the twentieth century, however, movements to standardize and professionalize the social services began in earnest. Catholics involved in community work realized that the Church would have to follow suit in order to be taken as a serious and acceptable alternative to secular social and charitable services or those of other religious traditions. In some cities, such as Baltimore and New York, Catholic volunteers and social workers who worked through their parishes or dioceses also had seen the benefits of coordinating efforts across localities to pool resources, prevent duplication, and provide better, standardized services.

In response to emerging Catholic social teachings, such as Leo XIII's 1891 encyclical *Rerum Novarum* (On the Condition of Labor), and to secular and other religious, political, and social movements, Catholic social workers and volunteers increasingly looked beyond charitable provision to campaigning for social justice. Many came to see that their work should embrace not only charity but a campaign for improved living conditions in the form of fair wages and shorter hours, child labor laws, improvements in public health, social insurance, and working conditions.

In 1910, the Church's need to establish a more effective mechanism to undertake large-scale enterprises in social services prompted the first formal meeting of American bishops since the Plenary Council of Baltimore in 1884. Just as the 1884 meeting placed a priority on expanding Catholic education, the 1910 meeting was focused on the charitable work of the Church. Bishops, clergy, and laity gathered at the Catholic University of America in Washington, D.C., to found the National Conference of Catholic Charities (NCCC). Their primary goal was to unify existing Catholic charitable organizations and institutions by coordinating existing efforts and creating standards of practice and service. A second goal was to build on Catholic social thought by establishing a Catholic theory of social work and training Catholics to integrate their religious principles into the provision of social services, whether as diocesan priests or administrators of charitable organizations, members of religious orders, lay social workers, or volunteers.

Again, war provided an impetus to organize along broader lines as Catholics were drawn into military and medical service as well as industrial work during World War I. The National Catholic War Council was founded in 1917 to coordinate Catholic fundraising and overseas services, overseeing the work of thousands of lay volunteers. This effective national network was transformed in 1919 into a permanent organization, the National Catholic Welfare Council, which became the National Catholic Welfare Conference (NCWC) in 1921. "Welfare" was inserted into the organization's name because it encompassed the broad goals of the Church in general – a concern to provide for Catholic well-being through charitable social services, and the inclusion of the maintenance of a specific religious identity and perspective within those services.

Volunteers, in great part women, made up the majority of those working in the different associations that were part of the Catholic charities network. As a result, the National Council of Catholic Women (NCCW) became the first unit organized in the NCWC's Department of Lay Organizations, building on previous efforts to coordinate the activities of Catholic women's organizations before and during World War I.

The need to professionalize social services prompted the foundation of numerous programs of study of social services at Catholic colleges and universities between 1910 and 1940. Initially intended to prepare seminarians for the social aspect of their vocation, these programs of study in social science and social work were expanded to include lay students.

Responding to the growing number of women interested in participating in volunteer and professional social service work, the NCCW sponsored a separate National Catholic School of Social Service (NCSSS) at the Catholic University of America. Although originally intended to train lay women to volunteer alongside diocesan priests and coordinators of charities, the NCSSS became an accredited program of social work, the graduates of which went on to work in salaried positions in Catholic organizations, and also in public and private agencies.[4]

During the Great Depression, the Catholic Church provided one of the first and largest charitable networks to respond to nationwide crises following the 1929 stock market crash. Catholics were involved in both relief and policy work, through organizations such as the NCWC, the Society of St. Vincent de Paul, the Ladies of Charity, Big Brother and Big Sister organizations, the Catholic Daughters of America, and through diocesan and parish programs. Catholic professionals from universities, social service organizations, and public agencies served on presidential committees and in national, state, and local relief programs.

Catholic leaders were instrumental in shaping some of the legislation of the New Deal – for example, New Yorker Jane Hoey was appointed assistant director of the New York City Welfare Council and then as director of the Bureau of Public Assistance under Franklin D. Roosevelt – ensuring that public provision of social services and funds did not conflict with or render obsolete private and religious charities (for example, the provision of Aid to Dependent Children was restricted to blood relatives, thus preserving natural family ties and preventing the removal of Catholic children from their home environment to perhaps non-Catholic ones). Catholic leaders also argued, with limited success, for the provision of public funds to faith-based organizations, given the extent of the latter in communities nationwide.

Also during this time, U.S. Catholics began turning their attention to international issues, especially when they involved countries to which they had ethnic ties. Catholic charities and volunteers mobilized in great numbers to raise funds and assist the war effort during World War II. Planning was also begun to address the problems of post-war famine, material deprivation, and dislocation, resulting in the establishment of a separate organization to address international concerns, Catholic Relief Services in 1943 (discussed below).

On the home front, many Catholic social services continued to be identified with movements for social reform. Through the 1950s, the NCCC placed great emphasis on social legislation to provide affordable housing, social security, child welfare, and other systems of support for the less advantaged. Once largely confined to urban settings, Catholic social services and relief programs began to extend into rural areas. The expansion of diocesan, parish, and organization programs renewed the need for volunteers to work alongside professionals and members of religious orders, who had come to lead many Catholic charitable institutions and services.

In this way, the work of Catholic charities paralleled the changes in American domestic policy, such as the War on Poverty, and those of the Second Vatican Council, in which the Church and its ministries reexamined their ethos and organization. In a reflection of the times, the NCWC was renamed the United States Catholic Conference (USCC) in 1966, putting its "national" identity in a global context.

A significant change that occurred during this time was the formal acknowledgment of the existing practice of the provision of services to non-Catholics. After a 1972 study, the NCCC renewed its mission "to provide quality services for people in need, to advocate for justice in social structures, and to call the entire Church and other people of good will to do the same."

In 1985, the NCCC also adopted a broader title, Catholic Charities USA. From 35 Catholic Charities bureaus in 1922, the Catholic Charities network has grown to over 1,400 agencies, institutions, and organizations today.[5] Since 1975, Catholic Charities has published an annual report of its services and personnel. Table 5.4 documents the growth of Catholic Charities USA since that time.

Table 5.4. Dioceses and Agencies Affiliated with Catholic Charities USA			
Year	Affiliated Dioceses	Affiliated Agencies	Individuals and Families Aided
1975	143	535	912,097
1980	150	740	2,808,916
1985	156	1,000	5,457,645
1990	158	1,200	8,199,429
1995	160	1,400	10,763,133
1997*	165	1,406	10,628,129
*Most recent year available			

Catholic Charities provides a broad range of social services to the community, including counseling, adoption and foster care services, migration and refugee resettlement services, and temporary shelter, food, and other emergency relief services.

Table 5.5. Personnel and Contributions to Catholic Charities USA		
Year	Paid and Volunteer Personnel	Income and Contributions
1975	88,692	$282,049,609
1980	112,193	$523,896,825
1985	150,823	$583,400,499
1990	218,001	$1,538,590,851
1995	301,722	$1,993,985,050
1997*	310,154	$2,273,961,690
*Most recent year available		

Catholic Charities USA aims to do more than carry out tasks or distribute funds. In working for both charity and justice, it includes a challenge for Catholics to see their society through the eyes of the less advantaged.

Catholic Campaign for Human Development

In addition to providing services directly, the Catholic Church in the U.S. also finances other organizations, in this way promoting smaller, community-oriented services that can respond to specific needs. The Catholic Campaign for Human Development (CCHD) has done exactly this by functioning as a funding agency that acts to promote organizations that embrace the principles of Catholic social teaching.

In 1969, the bishops of the United States acted on Pope Paul VI's mandate to "break the hellish circle of poverty" by establishing this domestic anti-poverty program. CCHD has two primary goals. The first is to raise funds to support self-help groups organized by the American poor that "develop economic strength and political power." The second is to sponsor educational programs to counteract negative stereotypes about the poor and to encourage those more affluent to support and act in solidarity with the poor. Rather than expecting that a Catholic organization alone could solve the problems of poverty, CCHD founders hoped that its funds would be used as seed money for other organizations of good will to create and assist programs to foster change. Although its focus is on communities in the United States, the CCHD forms part of the Vatican's international network Caritas Internationalis and the International Cooperation for Development and Solidarity (CIDSE).

Table 5.6. Catholic Campaign for Human Development Operating Expenses in 1999		
Program Expenses	**Total Spent**	**Percent**
238 Community Organizing Projects	$7,160,000	47%
62 Economic Development Projects	1,328,000	9
4 National Impact Projects	430,000	3
Welfare-to-Work Initiative	41,210	>1
Program Support	671,531	4
Education and Promotion	1,290,922	8
Administration	1,265,230	8
Reserved for Designated Funds	3,074,603	20

CCHD guidelines specify that projects must benefit a low-income community and at least 50 percent of project beneficiaries must be members of that community. Members of the group being served must participate actively in the project and in decision-making. The projects must conform to the moral and social teachings of the Catholic Church, aim to address the basic causes of poverty, effect institutional change, and "generally contribute to a more integrated and cooperative society."

Over three decades, the CCHD has funded more than 3,500 self-help projects developed by grassroots groups of low-income persons – Catholic, interfaith, and unaffiliated – distributing national grants to more than 275 projects based in local communities each year. Some of these projects are such well-known anti-poverty efforts as the Farm Labor Organizing Committee (FLOC), 9 to 5/Working Women, and ACORN (Association of Communities Organized for Reform Now).

CCHD-sponsored projects include voter registration drives; campaigns for legislation to improve health care, insurance coverage, wages, and working conditions; cleaning up neighborhoods and parks; initiatives to create jobs and increase investment in low-income neighborhoods, acquire funding for schools, improve police protection and provide for immigrants' rights. A 1994 Catholic University study concluded that these projects had affected "fully half of America's poor."

Supported solely by individual donations and grants, a mainstay of CCHD's financial support is an annual national collection, taken at every Sunday Mass in most dioceses on the Sunday before Thanksgiving. Consistent with the CCHD's preference to provide local solutions to local problems, the dioceses retain 25 percent of this collection to fund local projects.[6]

Led by a permanent committee of the USCCB and the CCHD advisory committee, the national staff manages day-to-day operations of CCHD's programs and activities. Diocesan CCHD directors, appointed by bishops, manage CCHD activities at the local level. Table 5.7 shows the number and distribution of CCHD personnel.

Table 5.7. Catholic Campaign for Human Development Personnel, 1999

	Religious			Lay		
	Men	Women	Deacons	Men	Women	Total
Advisory Committee	1	3	1	11	16	32
National Office Staff	1			6	7	14
Field Representatives				3	3	6
Diocesan Directors	42	27	1	59	46	175

OVERSEAS SERVICES

Catholic Relief Services

U.S. Catholic lay volunteers had mobilized to contribute to the support of soldiers, noncombatant medics and volunteers, and civilians in war-torn areas during World War I. The National Catholic War Council's Committee on Reconstruction and After-War Activities extended its overseas commitments to provide funding, supplies, and labor for famine relief, medical services, emergency shelter, and recreation centers until 1921, when it was reabsorbed into the National Catholic Welfare Council (NCWC). For the next two decades, the NCWC continued to receive requests for help from Catholics in other countries, whether from European countries suffering post-war famine, from those struggling to build newly independent or reorganized countries, like the Irish, those suffering religious persecution, as in Mexico, Spain, and the Soviet Union, or those fleeing fascist countries in Europe. The NCWC could not itself take up collections and at this point had no overseas relief budget. Instead, it responded by referring petitioners to individual Church leaders or associations for assistance. The NCWC also encouraged the bishops to authorize collections for overseas relief, even though the NCWC and the Church in general were already straining to deal with issues of poverty and injustice at home.

These services continued as the conflict in Europe escalated into World War II. As of 1939, the Catholic bishops made nationwide appeals for overseas aid, and the Bishops' War Emergency and Relief Committee was set up under the administration of the NCWC. Catholics again worked in conjunction with other groups such as the United Service Organization (USO) and ethnically based charities. In 1943, the Administrative Board of the NCWC voted to participate in the National War Fund of President Franklin D. Roosevelt's War Relief Control Board in order to make a single joint appeal to the American community for all war-related needs. This necessitated the creation of a distinct Catholic overseas aid agency that could care for both religious and material needs. First known as the War Relief Services of the NCWC, Catholic Relief Services was separately incorporated later that year. Its goal was to extend help to war-afflicted people, especially children, based solely on need, with no distinction of race, nationality, or creed.

While its first projects centered around aiding European refugees and victims of "natural and man-made disasters," CRS began to plan to provide international aid well before the war's end and soon broadened its vision to include supporting Catholic charitable works worldwide. Eileen Egan, who began working with CRS during World War II, was sent to Asia in 1955 to assess the roles that CRS could take in that region. Delayed in Calcutta, she was told to "go and meet Mother Teresa." This meeting sparked a 40-year relationship between CRS, the Missionaries of Charity, and other charitable organizations in India, Pakistan, and Bangladesh. Similar people-to-people encounters, coupled with rigorous research, accounting, and professional leadership, has enabled CRS to provide extensive service throughout Asia, Oceania, Africa, and Latin America.

Table 5.8. Catholic Relief Services Personnel, 1999				
	Priests/Men Religious	**Women Religious**	**Lay Men**	**Lay Women**	**Total**
Diocesan Directors	73	23	43	36	175
Board of Directors	13	0	0	0	13
Executive Officers	0	0	6	1	7
Directors of the Corporate Leadership Council	0	0	12	4	16
Country Reps. and Regional Directors	0	0	44	20	64

CRS is guided by a Board of Bishops and staffed by professionals committed to fulfilling the Catholic apostolate of helping those in need. CRS aims both to alleviate immediate suffering and to sponsor long-term, self-help programs that involve people and communities in their own development. To do so, CRS collaborates with both religious and secular groups. Nevertheless, it remains clear that the policies and projects sponsored by CRS must "reflect and express the teaching of the Catholic Church." CRS is funded through a national collection, the Annual Bishops' Overseas Appeal, through private contributions, and with U.S. government grants and agricultural commodities.

CRS's goals include the education of Catholics in the U.S. about international needs to encourage them to fulfill their moral obligation to alleviate suffering and help the poor. Some CRS campaigns familiar to many Catholics include: Operation Rice Bowl, the Lenten collection that since 1964 has raised money for overseas development projects and diocesan programs; the Food Fast Awareness Program in Catholic schools and other settings; and various programs to sponsor Catholic journalists, teachers, students, and others to visit CRS sites, host visitors from other countries, and generally expand awareness about the needs in other parts of the world and what Catholics can do to help alleviate them.[7]

Table 5.9. Catholic Relief Services Operating Expenses, 1999		
Program	**Cost**	**Percent**
Development Assistance	$84,826,000	34%
General Welfare	77,495,000	31
Disaster and Emergency Relief	54,426,000	22
Fund Raising and Awareness	12,583,000	5
Administration	11,166,000	4
Refugee Relief and Resettlement	7,647,000	3

Overseas Missions and Personnel

It was not until 1908, when Pius X promulgated the apostolic constitution *Sapienti Consilio* (On the Roman Curia), that the United States itself was removed formally from mission status. Before that time, and even into the 1920s, the Church in the United States received assistance from European Catholic mission-aid societies. As an immigrant country with a rapidly growing Catholic population, the U.S. has always been a net importer of priests, as it is today. During the nineteenth century, the mission focus of Catholics in the U.S. centered on evangelizing at home, mainly to European immigrants. Missions to Native Americans had existed in the Americas since the colonial period, and attention was turned to the U.S. Southwest after the Mexican-American War. The Spanish-American War also prompted the extension of U.S. missionary efforts to the Caribbean, via Cuba and Puerto Rico, and to Asia, via the Philippines. Efforts to establish home missions were extended to communities of African Americans and poor southern whites after the Civil War, and to Asian Americans, particularly in the West and in large cities in the East.

However, U.S. Catholics have demonstrated considerable enthusiasm for contributing to foreign missions for some time. The Society of the Divine Word, a German religious community of missionary priests and brothers, opened the first missionary seminary in the U.S., in operation in 1909 in Techny, outside of Chicago, Illinois. The first American missionary society, the Catholic Foreign Mission Society of America (more popularly known as the Maryknoll Fathers and Brothers), was founded in

1911, and sent its first priests to China in 1918. Women religious collaborated with Maryknoll's work from the start; the Foreign Mission Sisters of St. Dominic began in 1920 and in 1954 they were made a pontifical institute, the Maryknoll Sisters of St. Dominic. Missionary societies from Europe and other parts of the Americas also founded houses in the United States.

Missionary orders enjoyed an increasing membership for decades due to both the encouragement to increase missionary activity from Church leadership and the emergence of the United States as a world leader. In the 1950s and 1960s, the Catholic population of the U.S. was exhorted to support foreign missions, and in great part recognized and responded to this call, through organizations like the Catholic Student Mission Crusade and the United States Catholic Mission Association, a coordinating organization for communities and agencies.

The Second Vatican Council reiterated the necessity of baptism for salvation (*Lumen Gentium, The Dogmatic Constitution on the Church*). At this time, international concerns of some of the Catholic community also shifted from a broad-brush focus on anti-communism to increasing concerns about social development and world peace. Catholic missiona. ²s had been developing this emphasis on cross-cultural understanding and sensitivity towards political and social situations, long before they became more frequently discussed in Church discourse. The net result of all these developments was a renewed enthusiasm for missionary work, as well as a more nuanced appreciation of other cultures and histories, and concern to witness to justice and peace concerns overseas. The Catholic Church in the U.S. also became one of the world's strongest contributors to the Society for the Propagation of the Faith (also known by its Latin name, *Propaganda Fide*), and to relief organizations based at the Vatican and elsewhere.

The number of U.S. Catholics participating in foreign missions as priests, brothers, sisters, seminarians, and lay people peaked in 1968 at 9,655. While CRS has generally continued to grow as an international organizational presence, the number of Catholic missionary personnel has been declining since the late 1960s.[8] The presence of lay volunteers from the U.S. in foreign missions grew after World War II and through the 1960s and 1970s. Lay people joined the Papal Volunteers for Latin America campaign as well as the renewed efforts of other missionary societies. More recently, the number of lay missionaries affiliated with societies that are members of the United States Catholic Mission Association (USCMA) has also declined. However, it appears that the number of lay Catholics working in programs in foreign countries sponsored by individual parishes and other groups that are not affiliated with the USCMA has risen.[9]

Table 5.10. U.S. Overseas Missionaries					
	1960	**1970**	**1980**	**1990**	**1997**
Women Religious	2,827	3,824	2,592	2,347	1,513
Religious Priests	3,018	3,117	2,750	2,257	1,771
Brothers	575	666	592	477	347
Lay Persons	178	303	221	421	343
Seminarians	170	90	50	42	18
Diocesan Priests	14	373	188	200	172
TOTAL	6,782	8,373	6,393	5,744	4,164

Perhaps more important than the simple decline in numbers of overseas missionaries is an examination of the change in their composition. In 1960, 44 percent of those serving abroad were priests (religious and diocesan), 41 percent were women religious, eight percent were religious brothers, two percent were seminarians, and three percent were lay people.

Table 5.11. U.S. Catholic Missionaries by World Region, 1997			
Region	**Men**	**Women**	**Total**
Africa	449	350	799
Asia	612	280	892
Caribbean	209	151	360
Eurasia	8	4	12
Europe	85	87	172
Latin America	858	715	1,573
Middle East	45	16	61
North America	38	44	82
Pacific	149	64	213
TOTAL	2,453	1,711	4,164

The proportions that have changed most significantly are women religious, having dropped to 36 percent of U.S. Catholic missionaries overseas, and the number of seminarians, which dropped to less than half a percent. The proportion of lay people has increased more than three-fold, to eight percent. The percentage of priests has also increased somewhat, to 47 percent, while the percentage of religious brothers has remained stable, at eight percent.

As Table 5.10 shows, more than 4,000 Catholic missionaries from the United States serve around the world today.

CONCLUSION

Despite a century of change, the provision of Catholic charitable services and advocacy in crucial areas of health, social services, and overseas service remains central to U.S. Catholic activities. The nature of Catholic social and charitable work has changed due to the professionalization of social service work, changing standards, and the centralization of Catholic efforts, as services expand and problems become more complex. The vision of Catholic social service has also broadened, from primarily taking care of the Church's "own" to playing a major part in caring for the underprivileged in U.S. society. Catholic charitable institutions and agencies are well-distributed throughout the United States and serve large sectors of both the Catholic and non-Catholic population.

Like the Catholic educational system, Catholic charitable institutions have undergone significant changes in terms of their relationships with non-Catholic bodies. External sources of funding and cooperation with non-Catholic organizations or agencies have brought up new issues of identity, vision, and mission that Catholic charities have had to address. In 1998, the Campaign for Human Development changed its name to the *Catholic* Campaign for Human Development as a public reaffirmation of its origins and principles. The Catholic Healthcare Association launched a three-year initiative to formulate standards for Catholic health care providers, making room for both a Catholic identity and service to diverse communities.

War, famine, and economic crises, both within and outside the United States, have prompted Catholic leaders, priests, vowed religious, and lay people to work together in ways unimagined by their predecessors. In the mid-nineteenth century, Catholics who organized on the parochial level looked with suspicion on proposals to form national organizations. Today, organizations such as Catholic Charities USA, the Catholic Healthcare Association, the Catholic Campaign for Human Development, Catholic Relief Services, and the United States Catholic Mission Association benefit from pooled resources, exchange, and coordination. They also stand as members of international networks of Catholic agencies. Clergy and vowed religious are less common in leadership and direct service roles, but their efforts have been replaced by those of lay professionals – some of whom are committed Catholics – who have assumed a variety of leadership roles as their organizations have adapted and grown. The face of Catholic missions has changed, with a lessening of participation in programs sponsored by religious orders, and new developments in programs initiated by lay people and international service and relief organizations.

Over the past century, Catholic charitable organizations have adjusted to considerable social and organizational change. Nevertheless, at the beginning of the twenty-first century they continue to fulfill the same mission of alleviating human suffering as an integral part of practicing the Catholic faith.

PART III

Changes and Continuities in Catholic Ministry

The institutions designed to help the Catholic community gather and worship, pass on the faith, and promote the common good are served by people who themselves are part of networks and communities that contextualize the individual's response to God's call. Four major categories of ministers are examined in these final chapters: priests, religious, deacons, and lay ministers. Two of these categories – priests and deacons – are based on ordination. Also, with the exception of those priests who belong to religious communities, priests and deacons are selected and formed in institutions and programs established in their diocese or as determined by their diocesan bishop. Religious and lay ecclesial ministers have a different, less direct, relationship to diocesan structures.

Others, responding to God's call to formally consecrate themselves to vows of poverty, chastity, and obedience, enter particular religious communities, thereby participating in relationships and institutions that revolve around specific corporate commitments and spiritual traditions. These communities may be of local, national, or international scope, and may be concerned with a specific pastoral ministry or contemplative living, relatively removed from active engagement with the secular world.

New ways of thinking about deacons and lay ministers began to emerge as a result of the Second Vatican Council. Perhaps the greatest change concerns permanent deacons, reestablished as a permanent ministry in the Church by Paul VI in 1968.

Lay ministry has a much longer history in that anyone who is not ordained but performing a ministry function may be described as a "lay" minister, including vowed religious who are not ordained. After Vatican II, some ministry roles such as acolyte and lector, once reserved for ordained men as minor orders on the way to priesthood, were again counted as fully lay ministries. Many other contributions largely associated with laity, such as those of musicians and catechists, are also increasingly described as ministries. Many women religious pioneered lay service in these areas. Today, lay women and men who are not vowed religious make up the majority of lay ministers.

Priests and religious once managed and staffed virtually all Catholic programs, although many relied on important contributions from others. Today, lay ministers lead a significant number of Catholic parishes, schools, and other institutions and ministries. These trends have been growing in a way consistent both with Catholic tradition and specific teachings on the laity in contemporary Church life.

This third and final section examines the characteristics of and recent changes in the Church's pastoral workforce. Chapter 6 looks at priests, presenting the changing trends in clergy personnel throughout the twentieth century and assessing current available numbers of priests, both diocesan and religious, throughout the country. The chapter also examines trends in seminary enrollments.

Chapter 7 describes trends in vowed religious life in the United States. It examines trends in the numbers of women and men religious and presents the numbers engaged in various ministries in the Church today. A final section describes the communities of women and men that have been established in the United States over the past few decades.

The diaconate is examined in Chapter 8. This ministry has roots stretching back to the time of the apostles. The chapter explores trends in the numbers of those ordained to serve as deacons and in the programs that exist for those men preparing for the diaconate.

Chapter 9 concludes the section, and this volume, with a description of the emergence and growth of lay ecclesial ministry in the Church in the U.S. since Vatican II. It profiles professional lay ministers throughout the Church and the rich variety of ministries they perform. While varied, all provide ministry that responds to Christ's baptismal call.

CHAPTER 6

Priests

Priests are entrusted with parish and sacramental ministry, accountable to the diocesan bishop for local parish communities. Expectations regarding their ministry and life have changed as parish life has changed in size and scope over the past few decades along with parish life itself. The reasons for becoming a priest have not; priests of all ages report they entered the priesthood out of a desire to serve others, a deep love of the Eucharist, and an experience of God's call.[1]   Although the media tend to portray priests as beleaguered middle management, many surveys of priests consistently report high levels of satisfaction.

In the United States today, there are fewer priests in active ministry than in previous years, but more Catholics than ever before. These two facts are creating significant strains in both parish ministry and priestly life in parts of the country. However, while about three in four Catholics say they have noticed a decline in the number of Catholic priests over the last 30 years, less than one in four say they have been personally affected by this change.[2]   This may suggest that priests have absorbed the impact of declining numbers by assuming an increasingly heavy workload.

Chapter 1 discussed some of the factors relating to the increases in Catholic population in this century. This chapter discusses some of the demographic factors that have to do with the number of priests in the United States.

In 1900, there were approximately 12,000 priests in the United States, 75 percent of whom were diocesan priests. Fifty years later, that number had expanded to about 44,000, 63 percent of whom were diocesan. By the end of the century, priests numbered over 46,000, of whom 65 percent are diocesan. Expressed in terms of the number of Catholics, in 1900 there were 1,200 Catholics for each diocesan priest and 3,580 for each religious priest. By the end of the century, these figures had changed to 1,898 Catholics for each diocesan and 3,805 for each religious priest. However, whereas in previous years the percent of retired priests was negligible, the proportion of all priests estimated to be retired by 1998 is over 25 percent. This means that the effective change in the number of priests over this period is greater than the ratios above suggest. This does not include laicized priests, for whom data are not available.

In 1900, 43 percent of priests were concentrated in the Northeast, as were 51 percent of all Catholics. By the end of the century, 35 percent of all priests were in the Northeast, and the percent of all Catholics in that area had declined to 34 percent. This is partly a result of internal migration of Catholics from the North to the Sunbelt. It is also a result of massive Latin American immigration, particularly to Florida and the Southwest.

DIOCESAN AND RELIGIOUS PRIESTS

The number of diocesan priests increased steadily over much of the twentieth century, but in the 1970s their number began to slowly decline. By contrast, religious priests increased relatively slightly until about 1940.

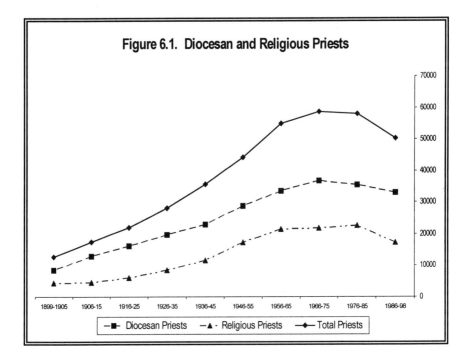

Figure 6.1. Diocesan and Religious Priests

Between 1940 and 1960 their numbers rose rapidly and then leveled off. By the late 1970s, the total number of religious priests began to decline at a rate faster than it had increased two decades earlier. While both diocesan and religious priests have declined in number over the past two decades, the pace of change for diocesan priests has been somewhat less pronounced, largely because the number of candidates to the religious priesthood has declined relatively faster.[3]

Of the more than 46,000 priests in the United States today, about 30,500 are diocesan and some 16,000 are religious priests. This includes all active and inactive (but not laicized) priests, both diocesan and religious. About one in four religious priests are active in parish or diocesan ministry. The remaining nearly 10,000 religious priests are active in institutional ministry, internal ministry, or other activities.

Religious priests make up about one-third of all priests in the United States. They comprise more than a third of the total priest population in the Northeast and a few other areas of the South and West. Religious priests are more than 40 percent of all priests in the South Atlantic and the Pacific regions.

However, for every religious candidate there are now about three diocesan priesthood students enrolled in theologates, which are Catholic graduate schools of theology required for ordination to priesthood. This is

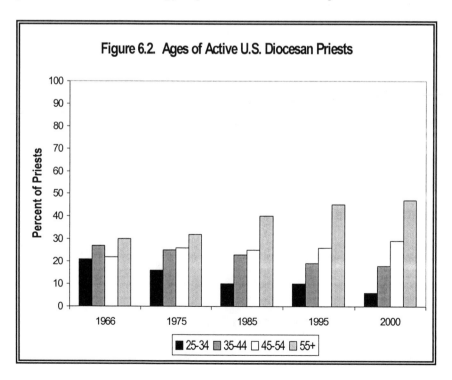

Figure 6.2. Ages of Active U.S. Diocesan Priests

in marked change to enrollments in the 1960s, when there was almost one religious for every diocesan candidate. As a result, the number of religious priests is likely to continue to decline at a faster rate than is the case for diocesan priests. Consequently, there will be more and more diocesan priests for each religious priest.

Ages of Diocesan Priests

Over the past 30 years, the percent of active diocesan priests between the ages of 25 and 34 has declined by half, while the percent over age 55 increased by 50 percent. Today, only about five percent of active priests are under age 35, while those over 55 comprise nearly half the total. These figures exclude retired priests and reflect estimates of active diocesan priests.[4]

Overall, the average age of diocesan priests in active ministry is 59, and that of active religious priests is 63.[5] In 1995, the average age was 58 for diocesan priests in active ministry and 61 for active religious priests. Figure 6.3 shows the approximate age distribution of diocesan priests as of 2000. As Figure 6.3 illustrates, two-thirds of diocesan priests are between the ages of 45 and 75. Fewer than one in five diocesan priests are under age 45.

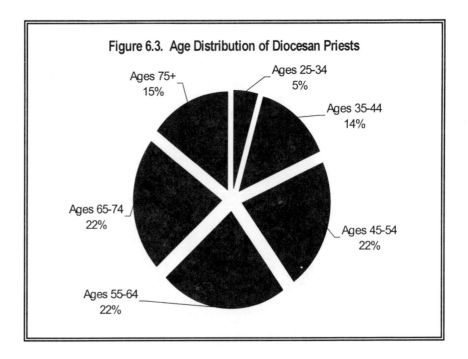

Figure 6.3. Age Distribution of Diocesan Priests

Ages 25-34 5%
Ages 35-44 14%
Ages 45-54 22%
Ages 55-64 22%
Ages 65-74 22%
Ages 75+ 15%

DIOCESAN PRIESTS ACTIVE IN MINISTRY

In 1999, the most recent year for which data are available, 22,394 diocesan priests out of a total of approximately 30,500 are reported by their dioceses as in active ministry. About 21,400 work in their home diocese, and another 2,500 work elsewhere, either in another U.S. diocese (about eight percent of all diocesan priests in the U.S.) or in a foreign mission assignment (a little under 200 diocesan priests from the U.S. serve in foreign missions). About two percent of priests in the United States are externs from a diocese outside the U.S., meaning that they are still formally part of a foreign home diocese.

Regionally, the Mid Atlantic Region (Region III, as discussed in Chapter 3), Upper Midwest Region (VII), New York Region (II), and New England Region (I) have the greatest numbers of both active diocesan priests and inactive diocesan priests. The South Atlantic Region (IV) has nearly three active for every retired or otherwise inactive priest. The most extreme situation is in the Northwest Region (XII) and the Upper Plains Region (VIII), where there are about two or fewer active priests for every retired priest. Other regions are somewhere between these two extremes.[6] Figure 6.4 shows the relative distribution of active and priests by USCCB region. For a complete description of the names and locations of these regions, see Table 3.3 in Chapter 3.

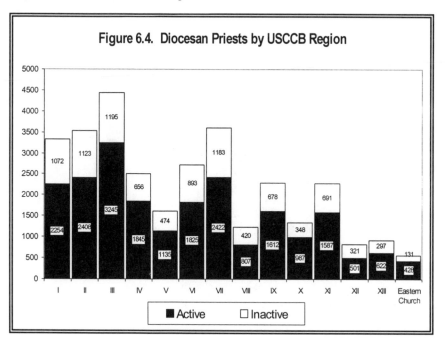

Figure 6.4. Diocesan Priests by USCCB Region

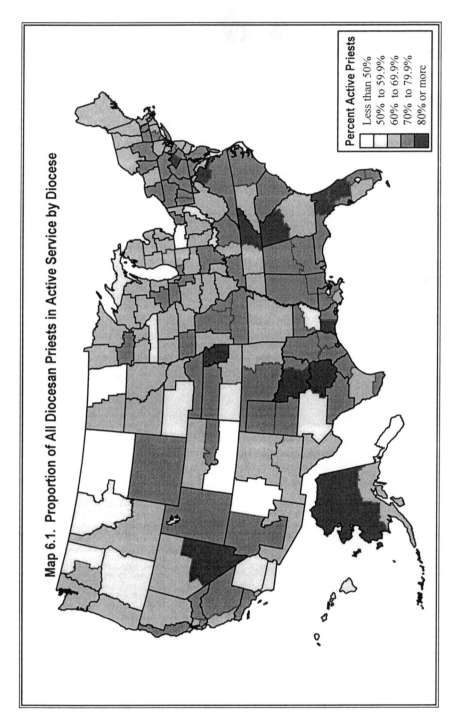

Map 6.1. Proportion of All Diocesan Priests in Active Service by Diocese

Percent Active Priests

Less than 50%
50% to 59.9%
60% to 69.9%
70% to 79.9%
80% or more

Map 6.1 shows the proportion of all diocesan priests who are in active service within each diocese. The dioceses shown in white have the smallest proportion of active diocesan clergy, but in many cases religious priests serving in parishes help make up for the shortage of active diocesan clergy.

As Figure 6.5 shows, close to 25 percent of the current diocesan presbyterate is retired, on leave, in full-time study, on sabbatical, or otherwise not actively engaged in full-time pastoral ministry.[7] Diocesan priests active in pastoral ministry in their home diocese comprise some 64 percent of the total diocesan priests engaged in active ministry.

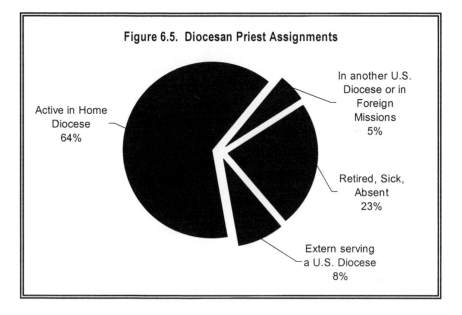

Figure 6.5. Diocesan Priest Assignments

In another U.S. Diocese or in Foreign Missions 5%

Active in Home Diocese 64%

Retired, Sick, Absent 23%

Extern serving a U.S. Diocese 8%

ORDINATIONS, DEATHS, AND DEPARTURES

The trend lines in Figure 6.6 illustrate the most important demographic factors affecting the numbers of diocesan priests. These three factors – ordinations, deaths, and departures from active ministry – provide much of the explanation for the "fewer priests" phenomenon now beginning to be experienced in many parts of the United States. The solid line in Figure 6.6 displays the net gain or loss of priests due to these changes. As the line goes down, it reflects a net loss in the total number of diocesan priests. When the line goes up, it reflects a net increase in the supply of priests. The other three lines describe how the trends in ordinations, deaths, and departures affect this net gain or loss.

Ordinations have declined sharply from their high point in the early 1960s, although this decline has slowed, beginning in the early 1980s. Deaths have increased steadily since their low point in the mid 1970s. Departures from the priesthood were at their highest between 1968 and 1972, but leveled off by the early 1980s. Since departures from the priesthood stabilized at that time, the net loss in numbers of diocesan priests in the 1980s and 1990s is now primarily due to fewer ordinations and more deaths.

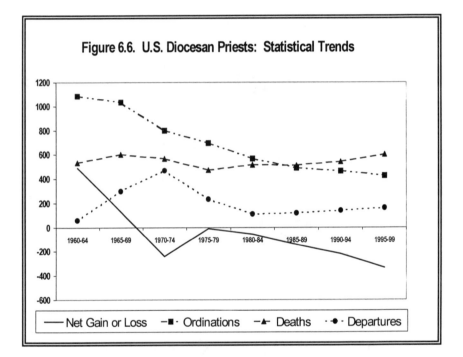

Figure 6.6. U.S. Diocesan Priests: Statistical Trends

Table 6.1 presents ordinations, deaths, and departures of all priests in the U.S. since 1960, with numbers projected for 2000 from extrapolations of the numbers of diocesan priests' ordinations, deaths, and departures.

Two factors cause growth in the number of priests in the United States: immigration of priests from outside the United States and ordinations of men as priests in the United States. The number of foreign-born priests today is about 2,400, and the largest groups are Irish (one-third of all foreign-born diocesan priests, although they largely immigrated decades ago), Vietnamese (eight percent), Filipino (eight percent), and Indian (seven percent).

Table 6.1. Ordinations, Deaths, and Departures of U.S. Priests				
Year	**Total Priests**	**Ordinations**	**Deaths**	**Departures**
1960	53,796	1,527	650	75
1965	57,730	1,575	725	125
1970	59,434	1,245	750	675
1975	58,255	1,136	850	425
1980	57,590	883	810	260
1985	56,132	748	905	230
1990	53,704	620	945	215
1995	50,753	520	965	265
1998	46,352	460	1,040	230

PRIESTLY FORMATION

The ordination of a priest is preceded by an extensive time of formation, typically eight years if he begins his studies immediately after high school or six years if he begins with a college degree in a field that would not have included the courses required to enter a Catholic theologate.

The final stage of priestly formation includes completion of the course of study in a theologate, or Catholic graduate school of theology. There are currently 46 such institutions in the U.S., of which 36 have largely diocesan and ten largely religious enrollments. In 1965, there were 134 of these institutions, and over 100 were primarily for religious. One of the greatest changes in the patterns of priestly formation in the U.S. has been the consolidation of religious seminaries over the past several decades.

Diocesan priesthood candidates typically live at the seminary and receive their education and priestly formation at the theologate they attend. Religious priesthood candidates today usually live in a house sponsored by their order and attend a nearby theologate for academic training.

The theologates with the ten highest enrollments account for 1,456 priesthood candidates, or more than 45 percent of total theologate enrollments. Table 6.2 lists these institutions in terms of total enrollments, as well as the numbers of diocesan or religious priesthood candidates enrolled.

Table 6.2. Theologates with Highest Enrollments, 1999-2000

Theologate	Priesthood Candidates		
	Diocesan	Religious	Total
Mundelein Seminary, IL	189	2	191
North American College, Rome	184	0	184
Mount St. Mary's Seminary, MD	165	3	168
Notre Dame Seminary, LA	128	22	150
Catholic Theological Union, IL	5	140	145
Immaculate Conception Seminary, NJ	107	25	132
Washington Theological Union, DC	1	106	107
Sacred Heart School of Theology, WI	98	4	102
St. Vincent Seminary, PA	74	23	97
St. Mary's Seminary and University, MD	90	0	90
Mt. Angel Seminary, OR	73	17	90

Seminary Enrollment Trends

Figures for seminary enrollments and seminarians provide a glimpse into the future of the priesthood in the United States. At the same time, of course, past numbers are no guarantee of future trends. Table 6.3 shows priesthood candidates already enrolled at theologates, providing some idea of the potential numbers of ordinations expected in the next four years. Of

Table 6.3. Theologate Enrollments in 1999-2000

Level	Expected Ordination	Priesthood Candidates		
		Diocesan	Religious	Total
4th year	2000	448	175	623
3rd year	2001	433	139	572
2nd year	2002	500	177	677
1st year	2003	487	185	672

course, ordination may be delayed or not occur altogether, but the numbers suggest that the supply of new priests will be steady.

Enrollments in theologates since 1965 have changed dramatically, as Figure 6.7 illustrates. These figures are for all theologates in the United

States or owned by U.S. bishops abroad, such as the North American College in Rome and the American College in Louvain, Belgium. They include a number of seminarians from foreign dioceses or foreign provinces of religious institutes – one-quarter of the 1999-2000 total – and therefore reflect more than the number of men who are candidates to serve as priests in the United States.

Theologate enrollments from 1968 to the present show steep declines from the beginning of the period through the end of the 1970s, as Figure 6.7 below illustrates.[8] The decline slowed through the 1980s; by the 1990s enrollments seem to have stabilized somewhat at about half the number of students enrolled at the beginning of this period. Closer analysis of the separate trend lines for diocesan and religious candidates reveal a sharp decline in vocations to the religious priesthood and a relatively softer decline in vocations to the diocesan priesthood.

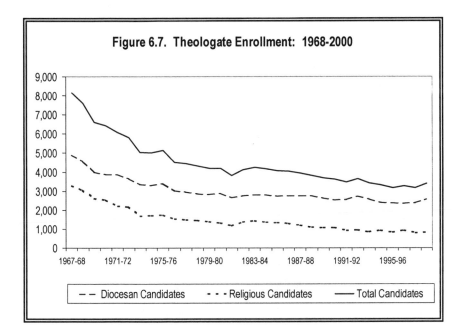

Figure 6.7. Theologate Enrollment: 1968-2000

Diocesan theologate enrollments have remained relatively stable throughout the 1980s and 1990s, with an average year-to-year decline of approximately one percent. Religious theologate enrollments, on the other hand, have continued to decline much faster, at a rate of about four percent per year throughout the same period.

The age distribution of seminarians is another important factor behind trends related to long-term changes in numbers of priests. In 2000, nearly 60 percent of seminarians in theologates are over age 30. As with other religious bodies, the majority of Catholic priesthood candidates are now increasingly "non-traditional" students in that they have not begun studies for the priesthood immediately upon completion of their undergraduate degree.

This is in contrast to many of today's older priests, who entered a high school seminary and proceeded to a college seminary (both "minor" seminaries), and then to theologate (or "major" seminary), often on the same campus. The effect of later ages of ordination is being felt in a number of ways. If the average age at ordination is some ten years later, a diocese or religious order will have the benefit of ten fewer years of active ministry. It also means that the relative age distribution of the priesthood is likely to continue to be concentrated in the older age groups. This trend will have long-term implications for the supply of priests available to serve. Even if the number of seminarians continues steady or increases gradually, as it has in the past five years, they will not be enough to replace the older priests who are retiring, and thus will not substantially affect the total number of active priests.

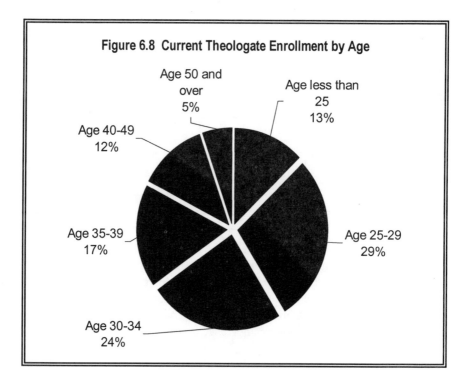

Figure 6.8 Current Theologate Enrollment by Age

Age 50 and over 5%

Age less than 25 13%

Age 40-49 12%

Age 35-39 17%

Age 25-29 29%

Age 30-34 24%

PARISHES WITHOUT A RESIDENT PASTOR

One of the consequences of having more Catholics and fewer priests is that dioceses now face the problem of too few active priests available to administer parishes. In 1960, there were approximately 500 parishes with no resident pastor. Today about 13 percent of parishes – nearly 2,500 – in the United States have no resident pastor. Figure 6.9 shows the distribution of parishes with no resident pastor by region. Map 6.2 also shows the percent distribution of parishes with no resident pastor by diocese.

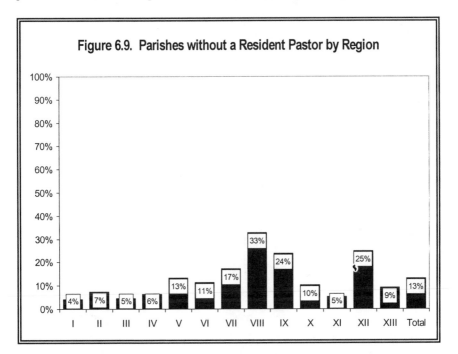

Figure 6.9. Parishes without a Resident Pastor by Region

Some of the interesting regional differences in the distribution of parishes without a resident pastor include:

- Nearly one-third of all parishes in the Upper Plains Region (VIII) have no resident pastor.

- The fewest parishes without resident pastors are along the East Coast and in the Northwest. Regions with fewer than 10 percent of these parishes include the New England Region (I), New York Region (II), Mid Atlantic Region (III), South Atlantic Region (IV), and Northwest Region (XII).

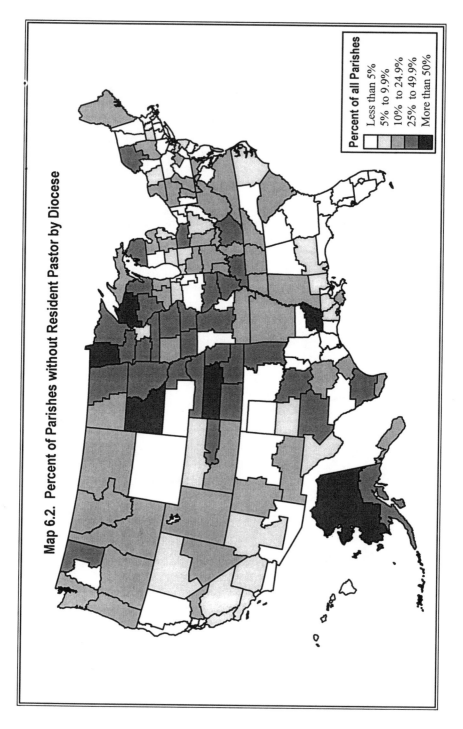

Map 6.2. Percent of Parishes without Resident Pastor by Diocese

Percent of all Parishes

Less than 5%
5% to 9.9%
10% to 24.9%
25% to 49.9%
More than 50%

- The Mountain Region (XIII) has the lowest absolute number of parishes without a resident pastor in a single region (60 parishes).

CONCLUSION

Priests are vital to the pastoral workforce of the Church, sacramental life, and parish leadership. Their numbers grew fairly steadily in the first six decades of the century, but began to drop somewhat as ordinations declined over the past three decades.

Although fewer priests are available for ministry today, the sacramental needs of Catholics continue to be met, though how much of this need is met by priests absorbing the workloads of several priests in the pastoral ministry cannot be determined. Clearly, the challenge in a time of fewer priests is to increase new priestly vocations while supporting those currently serving in priestly ministries, whose modeling and lived witness of priestly life is essential to cultivating vocations of future priests.

Increasingly, providing for pastoral needs during a time of limited numbers of priests suggests that emerging patterns of collaboration with deacons, lay ecclesial ministers, and others will continue to be important to the Church in the future.

Central to any response to issues of fewer priests in the U.S. today will be a consideration of the relationship of priests to all aspects of the Church's workforce. The chapters that follow consider other ministers, such as vowed religious, deacons, and lay ecclesial ministers, who share a vocation to Church service.

CHAPTER 7

Religious Priests, Brothers, and Sisters

A religious institute is "a society in which members . . . pronounce public vows . . . and lead a life of brothers or sisters in common" (c. 607.2). Religious vows are different from ordination, since they involve a consecration of life rather than the sacrament of holy orders. Members typically take the vows of poverty, chastity, and obedience – the "evangelical counsels" or moral ideals Jesus set out in the Gospel – with the goal of living them out to their fullest. Their vows do not change their identity as laity within the Church, although some men religious can also be ordained priests if they pursue priesthood formation.

Properly, the term "religious institute" is the more inclusive for the various communities of women and men religious. The term "religious orders," although often used as synonymous with "religious institutes" or "religious life," technically refers to a former distinction in canon law. Orders are older (the last one was founded in 1752), and initially were relatively more prestigious. Their members took the more binding and formalized "solemn vows."

Other religious institutes were founded as "congregations," communities whose members took "simple vows." Members of religious institutes taking simple vows were at greater liberty to perform acts of charity because they were not bound to cloister rules. In the spirit of the renewal of religious life promulgated in the Vatican II document *Perfectae Caritatis* (Decree on the Appropriate Renewal of Religious Life), this distinction was completely eliminated. The 1983 Code of Canon Law uses the term "perpetual vows" without distinction.

Perfectae Caritatis called for religious institutes to review their constitutions with two distinct but complementary goals. First, they were to return to "the sources of all Christian life" and to the intentions of their founders for inspiration. At the same time, they were to find ways to adapt to the "changed conditions of our time." This led to such visible changes as the adoption of much less distinctive dress and less structured forms of community living as well as more fundamental changes in the constitutions and internal codes of religious institutes.

Historically, a relatively small minority of religious institutes in the United States follow a contemplative monastic tradition. The vast majority, 95 percent, are actively engaged in religious ministry, such as parish work, teaching, health care, or social services. However, many of these communities incorporate elements of contemplative monasticism into their common life.[1]

Religious institutes can be diocesan, meaning that they are closely linked to the supervision of their local bishops, or pontifical, meaning that in some respects they are directly under the leadership of the Pope. Some religious institutes are, or were in their early stages of formation, "pious societies." These kinds of entities require no special vows of their members, but need the approval of their local bishop or a higher Church authority to operate as a distinct religious community within the Church.[2]

Often the more imprecise term "community" is used instead of religious institute, order, or congregation, since it describes the kind of relationship a religious institute represents. It is also common to refer to "religious life," and its members as "religious." However, the most precise term is "consecrated life," since members of religious institutes are distinguished for having taken public vows consecrating themselves to God and the evangelical counsels in a special way, committing themselves to a community-based relationship with other members of their institute as brothers or sisters in Christ. Those consecrated to contemplative orders are "monks" and "nuns"; members of active religious orders are more commonly known as "brothers" and "sisters," but often no real distinction is made in the common use of these terms.

These women and men have been the major source of the pastoral labor force for most of the history of the Catholic Church in the U.S. Religious priests and brothers have been present since the very beginning of European settlement in North America, when they established missions for the proselytization of Native Americans and staffed the first parishes and schools. The first bishop of a diocese in the U.S., John Carroll, himself had taken vows as a Jesuit, as had most priests who served in the original thirteen colonies.

Women religious have played a vital role of service to the Church in the United States. The first foundations of sisters in what would become the U.S. appeared in the eighteenth century. The Ursuline Sisters were established in New Orleans in 1727, the Discalced Carmelite Nuns in Port Tobacco, Maryland, in 1790, and the Visitation Nuns in Georgetown (later Washington, D.C.) in 1799.

The first U.S.-founded community, the Sisters of Charity of St. Joseph, was begun in 1809 by St. Elizabeth Seton. During the past two centuries, more than 100 communities of women religious have been founded in the U.S., primarily to work with the poor, the uneducated, the sick, the enslaved, and other marginalized populations. From the late nineteenth century onward, the numbers of women religious engaged in ministries eclipsed that of priests and brothers.

In addition, hundreds of congregations of women religious that were founded in Europe established themselves in the U.S., including what is now the largest single religious institute of women in the U.S., the Sisters of Mercy, established in Ireland by St. Catherine McAuley in 1831. The women who belonged to this rich variety of communities and spiritual traditions became pioneers in establishing institutions and providing services that built up the Church from the grassroots in the United States. Their contributions in education, health care, and other charitable institutions have been explored in earlier chapters.

This chapter presents trends in vowed religious in the United States, including some findings on emerging religious communities.

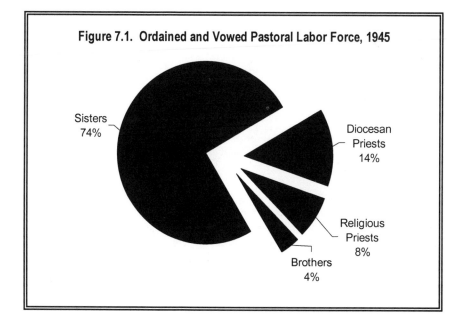

Figure 7.1. Ordained and Vowed Pastoral Labor Force, 1945

Sisters 74%

Diocesan Priests 14%

Religious Priests 8%

Brothers 4%

RELIGIOUS LIFE IN THE U. S. AT MID-CENTURY

The first date for which complete membership figures exist for religious priests, brothers, and sisters in the United States is 1945. At that time, there were some 12,800 religious priests, 6,500 religious brothers and nearly 140,000 religious sisters for the 24.5 million Catholics in the United States. In other words, in 1945 there were 1,900 Catholics for every religious priest, 3,800 Catholics for every religious brother, and 175 Catholics for every religious woman.

At this time, deacons did not exist outside the transitional diaconate to which men were ordained on the way to priesthood, except in some Eastern Churches. Non-vowed lay pastoral staff in parishes, and even non-vowed lay teachers in Catholic schools were rare. The Church pastoral workforce was comprised almost exclusively of women and men religious and diocesan priests. As Figure 7.1 shows, Church personnel was predominantly composed of members of institutes of consecrated life, particularly women.

Table 7.1. Women and Men Religious: 1945-1998				
	1945	**1965**	**1985**	**1998** **Change** **1965-98**
Religious Priests	12,413	21,781	20,448	15,024 -31%
Religious Brothers	7,003	13,152	10,226	6,054 -54%
Religious Sisters	122,159	173,865	118,840	83,302 -52%
Catholics (millions)	21.9	41.5	148.4	52.3 26%
Catholics Per:				
Religious Priest	1,767	1,907	2,368	3,485 83%
Religious Brother	3,132	3,157	4,735	8,648 174%
Religious Sister	180	239	407	628 163%

The period of most rapid growth in vowed religious life was between 1945 and 1965. The number of sisters peaked in 1965 at 181,421. Religious brothers peaked the next year at 12,539, and religious priests reached a peak of 23,021 in 1967.[3]

The last column of Table 7.1 compares the peak of vowed religious life in 1965 with figures for 1998 and demonstrates just how striking the change has been over the past three decades.[4]

Religious Priests

During the twentieth century, absolute numbers of vowed religious priests first increased slowly, then rapidly, and then began to decline from about 1980 onward. While there are still more than three times the number of religious priests than at the turn of the twentieth century, the number of Catholics is nearly six times higher than 100 years earlier. Figure 7.2 shows the trend for religious priests during the twentieth century.

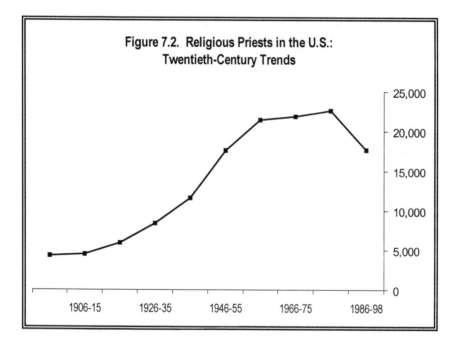

Figure 7.2. Religious Priests in the U.S.: Twentieth-Century Trends

Religious Brothers

Relatively few separate statistics exist on religious brothers in the early U.S., but their numbers can be documented since 1945. Like religious priests, their number peaked in 1966 and has steadily declined since that time. Figure 7.3 shows the growth and decline in numbers of religious brothers in the United States between 1945 and 1998.

Map 7.1 shows the distribution of men religious – both religious brothers and religious priests – around the country by state. As the map shows, men religious are still concentrated in areas where they have had a strong presence, such as the Northeast, the Midwest, and the Southwest. But religious brothers and priests also provide an important ministry presence in other areas, such as the rural South and the Northwest.

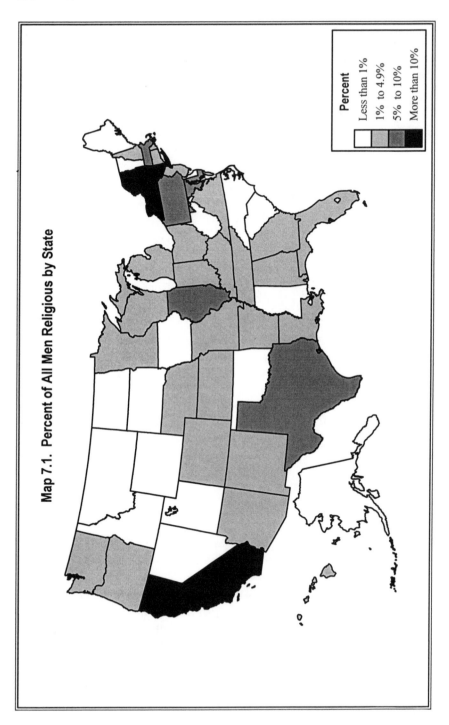

Map 7.1. Percent of All Men Religious by State

Percent

Less than 1%

1% to 4.9%

5% to 10%

More than 10%

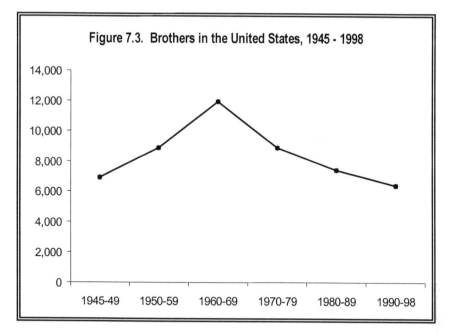

Figure 7.3. Brothers in the United States, 1945 - 1998

Women Religious

The numbers of women religious show a similar pattern, although in this case one can document a drastic increase from the late nineteenth century through the mid-twentieth century, followed by a continued increase after World War II and a sharp decline since the mid-1970s. Figure 7.4 takes the numbers of women religious back to the early nineteenth century, when they first became a sizeable presence in the United States.

Comparing the numbers of religious to the total number of Catholics in the population provides a more nuanced portrait. For example, the number of Catholics per sister is very similar now to the number 150 years ago (610 Catholics for every sister in 1860, compared with 672 in 1998). Worldwide, the present ratio of Catholics per sister is 674 in Oceania, 729 in Europe, 823 in Asia, 3,320 in Latin America, and 2,264 in Africa.[5]

Growth and Contraction in Membership

A cyclical pattern in religious life is well-documented. Many of the contemplative and cloistered religious orders founded during the Middle Ages had all but disappeared by 1850 as a result of European revolutions, Church-state conflicts, and the general anti-clericalism of the age. During the nineteenth and twentieth centuries, in the U.S. as well as in other parts of the world, numerous religious orders were founded that could address contemporary social problems, such as the growing need for education,

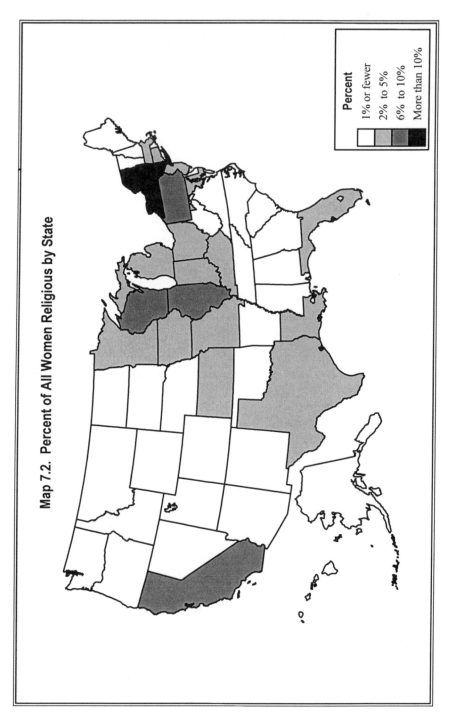

Map 7.2. Percent of All Women Religious by State

Percent

1% or fewer
2% to 5%
6% to 10%
More than 10%

medical care, and other social services. The increase in the numbers of vowed religious in the U.S. was also related to the presence of large immigrant populations, which both offered fields for ministry and potential new members. Some older, established orders enjoyed a revival in places where social tensions had eased. Many newer institutes were also created in response to the needs of the time. Women especially found new opportunities for active ministry not present in earlier cloistered communities. For more than a century, women and men religious formed the backbone of the Catholic school system, Catholic health care system, Catholic charitable services, and missionary movements in the U.S.

After the Second Vatican Council, the Church urged religious communities to renew themselves in light of the original intent of their founders and the signs of the times, leading many communities to explore new ways of living out their lives and their commitments. Such a serious spirit of renewal led some to consider even whether they were indeed called to remain in vowed life. These reflections resulted in the exit of a considerable number of women and men from vowed religious life, although many continued to serve the Church in some form of lay ministry. At the same time, the Church encouraged laity outside of religious life to take on many ministries that had previously been seen reserved to vowed religious or priests. Thus many who felt a vocation for pastoral ministry in Catholic schools, social services, and parishes came to view the vowed

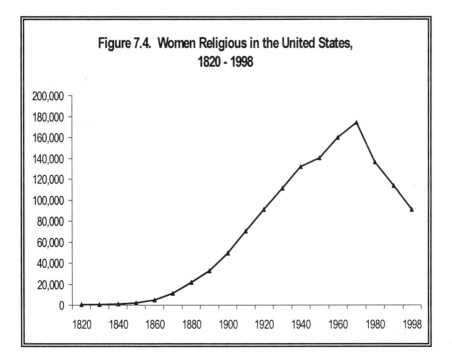

Figure 7.4. Women Religious in the United States, 1820 - 1998

life as only one way that people other than priests could enter into these forms of Christian service.

As a result of these changes, consecrated life today is coming to be focused more towards issues of spirituality and community building than exercising particular ministries or serving specific institutional needs of the Church. New members of religious institutes know that they can perform a variety of ministries outside of religious life but find that religious life offers the unique support of a community and living spiritual tradition.

Today, there are some 103,000 vowed religious in the United States. Approximately 21,000 (20 percent) are men, and about 82,000 (80 percent) are women. Of the men, about 15,400 or 73 percent are priests, and about 5,700 or 27 percent are brothers.

Average Age
The median age of religious sisters in 1998 is 68, meaning that half of all sisters are older than 68. Table 7.2 shows how the median age differs slightly for religious women, depending on whether they belong to active or contemplative communities.[6]

Table 7.2. Median Ages of Women Religious				
	1985	**1989**	**1993**	**1997**
Active	63	65	67	69
Contemplative	62	63	64	65

Men religious, on the other hand, have approximately the same median age, regardless of whether their primary lifestyle is active or contemplative.

Table 7.3. Median Ages of Men Religious				
	1985	**1989**	**1993**	**1997**
Active	54	57	59	61
Contemplative	55	57	58	61

The median age of religious priests in 1998 is 62.[7] That is, half of the more than 15,000 religious priests are older than 62 and half are under this retirement age traditional for secular employment. "Retirement," however, has a different meaning for religious. Since the consecrated life is a lifelong commitment rather than a career, "retirement" often means having somewhat fewer responsibilities, rather than a complete break with one's ministry in life.

Racial and Ethnic Background of Today's Religious

The overwhelming majority of religious in the United States today are white. About one percent of vowed religious are African American, another one percent are Asian, and about two percent are Hispanic/Latino. However, a much greater proportion of new members of religious communities are non-white. According to a 1993 study of initial formation in communities of women and men religious having central houses and/or houses of formation in the U.S., 71 percent of women in temporary vows were white, two percent were black, 16 percent were Hispanic/Latina, and 11 percent were Asian. The proportion of minorities was even greater in the earlier levels of religious training.

The same held true for men in temporary vows in clerical religious institutes (men's communities that include priests) where 74 percent were white, four percent were black, 11 percent were Hispanic/Latino, and 11 percent were Asian. A somewhat higher proportion of men in temporary vows in institutes of religious brothers were white – 83 percent. Eight percent were black, four percent Hispanic/Latino, 11 percent Asian, and one percent Native American.

In addition, many foreign-born religious serve in the U.S., especially European-born religious priests. Just over 1,000 religious priests serving in parish or diocesan ministry are foreign-born. Most come from Europe, although India, Canada, and Mexico, among others, have also contributed significant numbers of religious priests who fulfill their vocation in the United States.

NUMBER AND TYPES OF COMMUNITIES

Active Ministries of Vowed Religious

Religious are engaged in a broad variety of ministries within the Church. Over 4,600 religious priests work in parishes and diocesan offices. Some 375 brothers and 6,600 sisters are employed as pastoral ministers in parishes. Another 1,900 religious priests, 1,100 brothers and about 9,200 sisters are engaged in teaching.[8] Some 1,700 religious priests, 1,500 religious sisters and about 350 religious brothers serve in foreign missions.[9]

Table 7.4 shows the relative distribution of sisters, priests, and brothers in each of the major ministry areas.[10]

	Priests		Brothers		Sisters	
Table 7.4. Vowed Workforce in Major Ministry Areas Absolute Numbers and Percentages for Priests, Brothers, and Sisters						
Parish/Diocesan	4,621	56%	375	20%	6,600	26%
Education	1,900	23%	1,114	61%	9,200	37%
Health Care	N/A		N/A		7,862	31%
Foreign Missions	1,736	21%	347	19%	1,513	6%
Total	8,257		1,836		25,175	

Societies of Apostolic Life

Another, special category, Societies of Apostolic Life (c. 731-746), includes such communities as the Maryknoll Missioners, the Columbans, the Missionaries of Africa, and others. These societies of men and women were founded primarily in the nineteenth and early twentieth century. They do not necessarily require all their members to take religious vows of poverty, chastity, and obedience, and therefore are technically not religious institutes. Instead, their members and are joined by an oath of community and a commitment to a common ministry, primarily the missions. In the United States there are fewer than two dozen of these societies.

EMERGING RELIGIOUS COMMUNITIES

Since 1960, 147 new religious communities have been organized in the United States. Two-thirds of these communities have been organized in the past two decades. Many are in various stages of formal, canonical recognition. More than three-fourths have attained some form of canonical status, and another 15 percent are seeking official recognition by the Church.[11]

Of the total number of emerging religious communities found in a 1998 study, 136 are native to the U.S. and 33 are local houses of communities or movements that originated in other countries. They are distributed in 87 dioceses and eparchies in 38 states and the District of Columbia. Some 48 of these groups admit only men, 66 admit only women, and 43 have mixed membership. Most of these new groups follow or plan to follow traditional models of religious life, including profession of public vows, the evangelical counsels of poverty, chastity, and obedience, and sharing in some kind of common life. Some adopt contemplative traditions, while others incorporate elements of these traditions into their community life.

However, not all of these communities are necessarily seeking to become institutes of consecrated life. Seven percent do not have and at present are not seeking any official status within the Church. Some can instead be classified as "Secular Institutes" (canon 710-730), a category formally recognized in 1947 in Pope Pius XII's *Provida Mater Ecclesia* (The Apostolic Constitution for Secular Institutes). Members of secular institutes are not necessarily celibate, do not necessarily live in community, and are not classified as belonging to a religious community. Instead, they strive to live out Christian perfection within themselves while acting as "leaven" in the secular world.

Some emerging communities of religious life include both vowed and non-vowed members or different forms of membership. Because they are still developing, many of these communities have not yet determined the type of community they hope to become or the ultimate status they seek within the Church.

Membership of Emerging Religious Communities

Forty-two percent of the emerging communities admit only women, 31 percent admit only men, and 27 percent admit both women and men to

Table 7.5. Profile of Emerging Religious Communities

	Percent
Men only	31%
Women only	42
Both women and men	27
Vowed only	67
Non-vowed only	9
Both vowed and non-vowed	24

membership. Two-thirds of the groups have only vowed members and one-fourth have both vowed and non-vowed members. About one-tenth have only non-vowed members. Six of the non-vowed groups are oratories of priests whose constitutions, modeled on those of St. Philip Neri, do not permit vows.

Spiritual Tradition of Emerging Religious Communities

About three-fourths of the communities follow a specific spiritual tradition. The most common are Franciscan (22 percent), Carmelite (12 percent), and Benedictine (11 percent). Other traditions these communities follow include Dominican, Ignatian, Salesian, and Augustinian as well as various combinations of these and other spiritualities. One-fourth of these new communities do not identify with any of the traditional spiritualities of religious communities, and instead say they have a new vision or spiritual focus not reflected in the older Catholic spiritual traditions described above. These communities tend to identify their basic charism, mission, or purpose according to one or more of the following broad headings: eremetic (those who live in smaller, more independent groups and devote themselves to contemplation and spiritual exercises), monastic (persons living in seclusion from the world, under religious vows and subject to a fixed rule of prayer, renunciation, and work), evangelizing (with a special focus on teaching prayer or doctrine), and apostolic (engaging in some specific form of pastoral ministry).

Size of Emerging Religious Communities

There are considerable variations among communities – and sometimes even within communities – in the degree to which members share in common life. Three-fourths of these communities report that all or some of the members live together. A similar percentage say that all or some of the members share funds in common. In most of these cases, only the full members and those in formation preparing to be full members live together and share funds in common.

As might be expected, groups of religious hermits, those who follow relatively solitary forms of contemplative religious life, are most likely to be small in membership – 90 percent have fewer than seven members. Almost three-fourths of emerging monastic groups also have fewer than seven members. Evangelizing and apostolic communities, on the other hand, are more likely to be relatively large: about half have seven or more members.

When it comes to the number of *new* entrants, evangelizing communities seem to be the most attractive. Over 90 percent have at least one person in formation for full membership. By comparison, 43 percent of the apostolic communities, 22 percent of the monasteries, and 30 percent of the groups of hermits report having no one in formation. Moreover, these latter types are also especially unlikely to have seven or more members in formation: only about one in ten of these communities report such figures. In contrast, almost half of the emerging communities that describe their mission as "evangelization" have seven or more persons in formation.

CONCLUSION

Religious life in the U.S. is changing in response to developments in the Catholic community and in society at large, but by no means is it disappearing. At the beginning of the twentieth century, its growth led to an enormous expansion of Catholic institutional life, notably in schools and charitable works. At the beginning of the twenty-first century, religious communities have largely passed on their institutions or have transformed them from a proprietary effort to a collaborative one.

Women religious served a vital role in carrying out these ministries. As lay people and as women within the Church and within the larger society they were pioneers. They built and operated complex organizations at a time when women had few leadership opportunities, acquired advanced levels of education when women had few educational opportunities, and then served in parishes and dioceses at a time when lay people had few ministry opportunities. Today, women religious continue to serve in these areas but are hardly limited to them.

Significantly fewer women and men are joining traditional religious institutes than in the past. A wide variety of new religious communities have emerged over recent decades. They are much more focused on community and spirituality than institutional life, as are many new members of the more traditional religious institutes. While their membership is much smaller than older, more established religious institutes at present, they reflect the increasing diversity of options available to Catholics seeking to fulfill a religious vocation.

CHAPTER 8

Deacons

The word "deacon" comes from *diakonia*, a Greek word meaning service. Deacons, *diakonoi* in Greek, were common in the first few centuries of Church life but gradually diminished in importance and eventually became simply a step on the way toward priestly ordination.

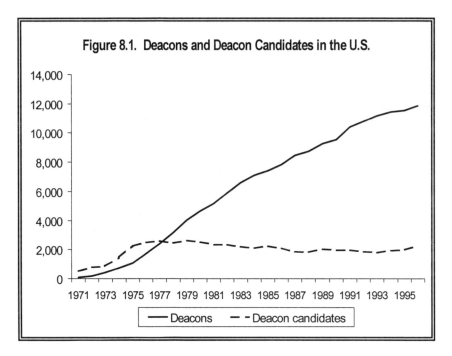

Figure 8.1. Deacons and Deacon Candidates in the U.S.

4 %
StL?

percent are African American, and less than one percent are Asian. The current enrollments suggest that deacons are growing in their racial and ethnic diversity.

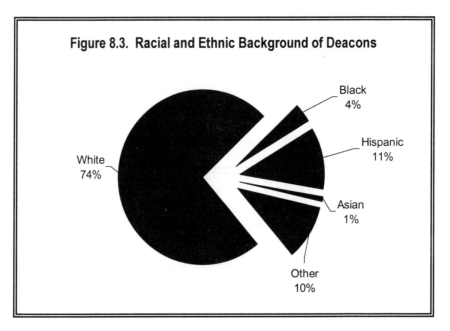

Figure 8.3. Racial and Ethnic Background of Deacons

White
74%

Black
4%

Hispanic
11%

Asian
1%

Other
10%

Some other characteristics of deacons include:

- More than nine in ten deacons are married. Only three percent have never been married.

- Deacons are well-educated compared to the population in general. More than 50 percent have a college degree and nearly 30 percent have a graduate degree in a secular field. By comparison, about 20 percent of all Catholics have a graduate degree.

Geographic Distribution of Deacons

Deacons presently serve in every state in the United States and the District of Columbia. They serve in nearly every diocese of the country as well. Only seven dioceses – Grand Island, Greensburg, Indianapolis, Kansas City in Kansas, Owensboro, Salina, and Worcester – report no deacons as of 1999, and some of these have begun formation programs. All but four jurisdictions of the Eastern Churches – Pittsburgh (Ruthenian), Our Lady of Deliverance of Newark (Syrian), St. Thomas the Apostle of Detroit (Chaldean), and the Armenian Exarchate – also have deacons.

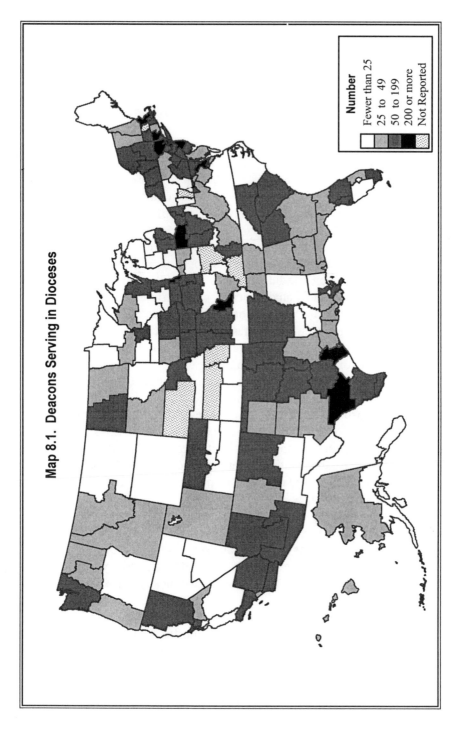

Map 8.1. Deacons Serving in Dioceses

Number

Fewer than 25
25 to 49
50 to 199
200 or more
Not Reported

Eleven dioceses have more than 200 deacons each. The Archdiocese of Chicago has 600, the highest number for any single diocese. Map 8.1 shows the distribution of deacons across the United States.

DEACON FORMATION PROGRAMS

Diaconate formation programs of some form currently exist in 45 of the 50 states. As of 2000, active programs exist in 127 of the 177 dioceses, and in 8 of the 15 eparchies of the Eastern Churches. At least 14 other dioceses are beginning, redesigning, or reactivating diaconate formation programs and consequently do not currently have candidates but will within the next year or two.

Diaconate formation programs differ in their requirements for admission, program duration, the number of required courses, the frequency with which candidates meet, and tuition and fees. Typical admission requirements include a period of discernment, recommendation by the candidate's pastor, the support of the candidate's wife (if married), letters of reference, psychological testing, and interviews. Although many programs do not specify academic prerequisites, some stipulate high school, college, or even graduate degrees.

Several dioceses offer separate English-language and Spanish-language programs or tracks and others conduct some of their classes in Spanish. A few provide instruction in other languages or train candidates to serve particular ethnic or cultural groups. The Diocese of Spokane, among others, makes special adaptations in its program for the culture and language of its Hispanic, Native American, and Asian participants, and the Archdiocese of Milwaukee conducts its program in English, Spanish, and American Sign Language.

Diaconate candidates typically meet one or two evenings or weekends a month over the course of four years, for an average of 187 hours annually. Some programs stipulate the prior completion of a lay ministry formation program. Program costs are often shared by participants, parishes, and dioceses, with the largest share typically paid by the diocese.

Age Distribution and Marital Status of Diaconate Candidates

As many as 75 percent of candidates for the diaconate are in their forties and fifties. Only about one in ten is under age 40, and one in five is over 60. This age distribution is markedly older than that of either priesthood candidates or lay ministry formation program participants. Many deacons have entered the diaconate after completion of a secular career. The vast majority of candidates – 95 percent – are married men.

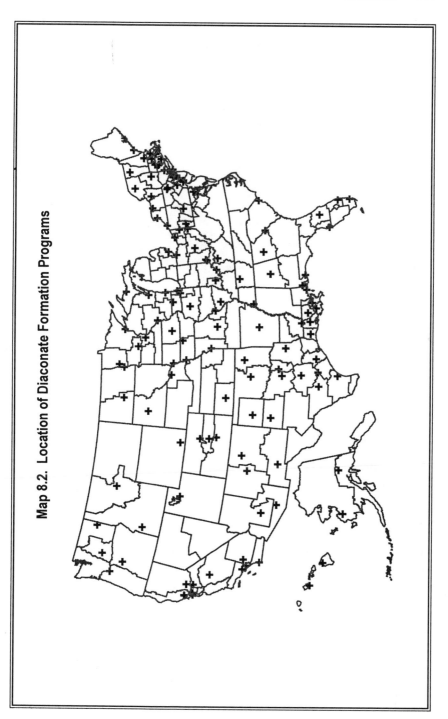

Map 8.2. Location of Diaconate Formation Programs

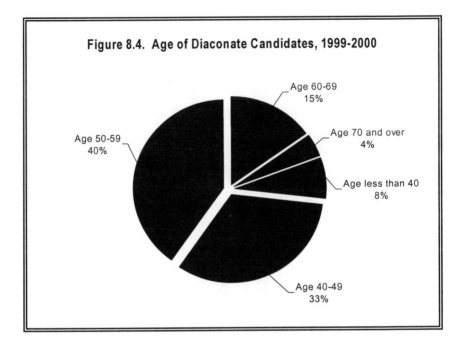

Figure 8.4. Age of Diaconate Candidates, 1999-2000

Age 60-69
15%

Age 70 and over
4%

Age 50-59
40%

Age less than 40
8%

Age 40-49
33%

Racial and Ethnic Background of Diaconate Candidates

Although a large majority of candidates are white, other racial and ethnic groups represent more than 20 percent of total enrollments in permanent diaconate programs. For deacons in formation in 1999-2000, whites are 79 percent of all deacon candidates, African Americans make up another four percent, Asians are approximately two percent, and Native Americans are a little under one percent.

Hispanics/Latinos form the largest minority group with 15 percent of enrollments, several percentage points higher than the current diocesan population. As for deacons in general, the ethnic and racial background of candidates is roughly comparable to that of the general Catholic population in the United States.

Educational Attainment of Diaconate Candidates

Almost 80 percent of current diaconate candidates have attended at least some college. One-third have college degrees and nearly one-fourth have graduate degrees. Figure 8.5 shows the complete educational profile of diaconate candidates in formation in 1999-2000.

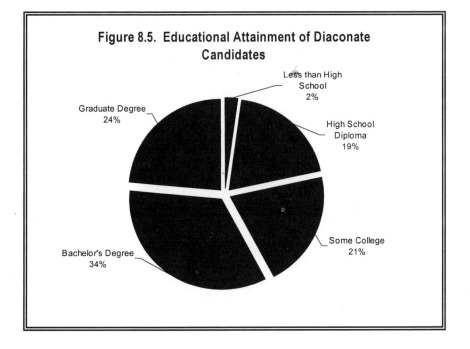

Figure 8.5. Educational Attainment of Diaconate Candidates

CONCLUSION

The number of deacons has grown dramatically over the past few decades. Those ordained to the order of deacon for permanent service in that role are now a large and established portion of the Catholic clergy in the United States. Most dioceses have or are planning formation programs to train deacons for the future.

Deacons now have a near-universal place in Catholic experience all over the country. In many ways, however, the diaconate is still a ministry in development, having only been present in its post-conciliar form in the U.S. for about three decades.

While deacons now comprise more than one in five of all ordained Catholic clergy in the United States, the ministry to which they are ordained is very distinct from the priesthood. The diaconate is a ministry of service that complements the ministries of priests and laity working together in Catholic parish and diocesan life.

CHAPTER 9

Lay Ecclesial Ministry

Perhaps the greatest change in Church personnel and in Church life during the twentieth century was in the area of lay ecclesial ministry. The Second Vatican Council specifically encouraged lay people to become active participants in the ministerial life of the Church. The response to this call has been impressive. Thousands of lay Catholics currently serve in professional ministry roles in the Church and many thousands more are in formation programs to prepare themselves for future Church leadership. Many more serve in a variety of liturgical ministries such as lector or Eucharistic minister. Until Vatican II, most of these ministries had been closed to laity. Those that were open to laity were often reserved for religious, or a preference was expressed for them, as in the case of religious education. Some of these roles, such as lector, had been named as one of the minor orders to which a man would be ordained on the way to priesthood. In 1972, these minor orders were suppressed and instead established as ministries open to laity. Many other ministerial roles, including service as an usher, organist, or music minister, and a variety of educational and service-related functions, had historically been filled by laity but became expanded and their importance emphasized during the 1970s and 1980s as new liturgical and pastoral needs emerged. Lay formation programs began to grow as bishops looked for ways to provide training for volunteers and meet needs for professionally trained ministers in a variety of fields.

The term "lay minister" applies to all forms of Church ministry and service exercised by laity, including teaching in Catholic schools and working in other Catholic institutions. The preferred term used to describe these new, professionally trained, long-term collaborators in parish and other related ministries is lay ecclesial minister. This term indicates that they are non-ordained Church ministries.

While the explosion in lay ministry has helped the Church provide new and more effective ministry precisely at a time when diocesan priests and religious were declining in number, the growth of lay ecclesial ministry is not primarily a response to these personnel needs. Rather, it comes from the Church's developing vision of itself as the Body of Christ. As then-president of the Bishops' Conference, Bishop Anthony M. Pilla, remarked in 1998:

> *I would like to dispose of the idea, often expressed, that this emphasis on the role of the laity is merely pragmatically useful, given the fewer priests in so many areas of our nation. While the laity have certainly helped cope with the situation, the renewal for their role is more than a pragmatic necessity. It springs from an interior renewal of the very meaning of what it is to be Church, in which we are guided by the Holy Spirit who renews the face of the earth.[1]*

Professional lay ministry formation programs are being developed in dioceses around the country to meet the demand for training lay persons who seek a more active participatory role in their Church. This chapter discusses the growth of lay ecclesial ministry since Vatican II and the variety of ministries entrusted to lay ministers. It also describes current lay ministry formation programs and the numbers of laity enrolled in them.

Most lay ecclesial ministers work in parishes, but some are diocesan employees and some work for other Church agencies. They are primarily paid, professional ministers, ordinarily employed by a diocese or parish.

As distinguished from ordained clergy, non-ordained members of religious communities are also laity. About 30 percent of lay ecclesial ministers are vowed religious, and almost all of these are women religious. Because they have a different relationship to Church life and apostolic service as a result of their vows, the focus of this chapter is primarily on these lay ecclesial ministers who do not belong to religious institutes.

Lay ecclesial ministers are often supported and encouraged in their ministry formation by their diocesan bishop. But that support is very different from his relationship to priests and deacons. Due to the relationship conferred by the sacrament of orders, priests and deacons are assigned to their pastoral ministry by their diocesan bishop and depend on the relationship with their bishop for the execution of their ministry.

Lay ecclesial ministers are also distinct from vowed religious who undertake ministries within a diocese at the invitation or permission of the bishop. Lay ecclesial ministers typically do not serve in a formal relationship with thé local diocese but rather are in an agreement with a particular parish or other unit of Church life. This, however, is changing in some dioceses that have centralized administrative aspects, or have consciously cultivated a sense of diocesan-wide connection among those in ministry.

Finally, lay ecclesial ministers are normally distinguished from parochial school staff, and other support staff such as secretaries and custodians, as discussed earlier. However, parish-based Directors of Religious Education (DREs), who provide Catholic education and formation in the context of parish religious education programs, are included here, together with parish youth ministers, pastoral associates, music ministers, liturgists, and a variety of others.

RECENT TRENDS

Professional lay employees existed in the Church before the Second Vatican Council, but they were almost always found in schools, hospitals, or other Catholic institutions. Lay persons played significant roles in Church life through a variety of men's and women's Catholic associations, such as the St. Vincent de Paul Society, the Knights of Columbus, and the Catholic Daughters of America. They also conducted youth programs, such as the Catholic Youth Organization, and maintained many ethnic and benevolent associations. But all of these activities were voluntary positions within the Church.

In the past few decades, lay persons have also become part of the formal leadership within parishes, serving as members of parish pastoral and

Table 9.1. Parish Lay Ecclesial Ministers		
	1992	**1997**
Vowed Religious	8,300	7,540
Lay Persons	11,700	18,460
TOTAL	20,000	26,000
Lay Ministers per Parish	1	1.4
Catholics per Lay Minister	2,820	2,258

finance councils and as pastoral ministers. Again, while these positions began as voluntary roles, parishes and dioceses have increasingly hired professional lay ecclesial ministers over the past few decades. More lay persons are now seeking formal training for professional lay ecclesial ministry than ever before.

More than 30,000 lay persons are currently enrolled in formation programs for professional lay ecclesial ministers. This figure illustrates the tremendous growth in lay ministry that has been developing for many years in parishes across the United States.

The numbers of professional lay ministers in parish and diocesan ministry relative to vowed religious personnel have also increased dramatically over the past twenty years. Table 9.1 demonstrates this change. The numbers given are for lay parish employees working at least 20 hours per week in pastoral positions.[2]

Some key trends in Catholic ministry personnel in the U.S. seen above in Table 9.1 include:

- The number of lay ecclesial ministers is increasing, and the number of parishes employing lay ecclesial ministers is also increasing. In 1992 about 54 percent of all parishes employed lay ministers. As of 1997 they are employed in nearly two-thirds (63 percent) of parishes.

- The number of vowed religious in parish lay ecclesial ministry is declining. Compared to 1992, there are more than twice the number of lay persons to religious in lay ecclesial ministry positions in 1997.

THE PRESENT SITUATION

Lay ecclesial ministry is open to all lay persons, but women provide most of the lay ecclesial ministry workforce in the Church today. Eighty-two percent of lay ecclesial ministers are women. One-fourth of these lay ecclesial ministers are women religious. As the number of sisters continues to decrease, lay women, and to a lesser extent lay men, are becoming involved in parish lay ministry. Among the lay ecclesial ministers who are not vowed religious, some two-thirds are married.

Ages of Lay Ecclesial Ministers

The average age of lay ecclesial ministers is 50, substantially younger than the average age of priests or deacons, whose average age is about 60, or vowed religious, whose average age approaches 70 years old. Compared to other lay ecclesial ministers, youth ministers tend to be even younger –

57 percent are under age 40 – and are more likely to be male. By contrast, more than half the pastoral coordinators and general pastoral ministers, who are usually women religious, are over age 50.

Table 9.2. Ages of Parish Lay Ecclesial Ministers Percent in each age group			
	Under 40	**40-60**	**Over 60**
Pastoral Coordinator	15%	54%	31%
General Parish Minister	8	45	47
Director of Religious Education	16	61	23
Coordinator of Religious Ed.	13	72	10
Liturgy Director	21	74	5
Music/Liturgy	25	75	--
Youth Minister	57	43	--

Racial and Ethnic Background of Lay Ecclesial Ministers

At present, most lay ministers are white, with minorities making up less than seven percent of lay ecclesial ministers. The figure below shows the racial and ethnic background of parish-based lay ecclesial ministers.

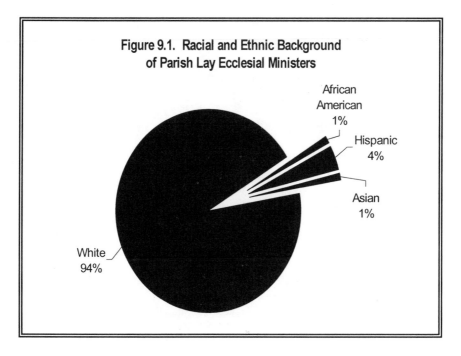

Figure 9.1. Racial and Ethnic Background of Parish Lay Ecclesial Ministers

African American 1%

Hispanic 4%

Asian 1%

White 94%

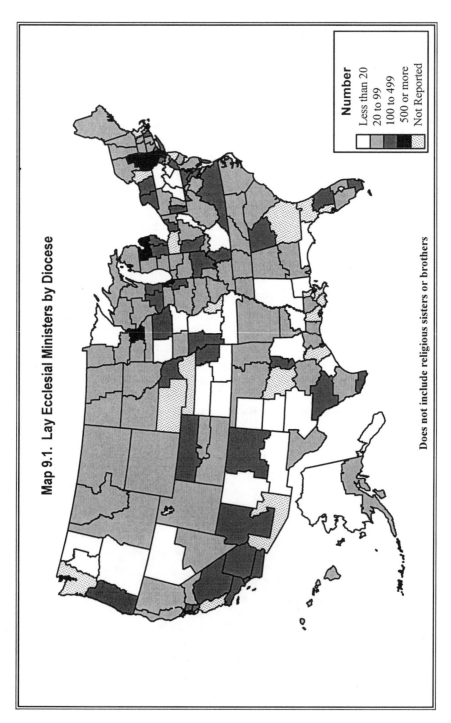

Map 9.1. Lay Ecclesial Ministers by Diocese

Number

Less than 20
20 to 99
100 to 499
500 or more
Not Reported

Does not include religious sisters or brothers

African Americans and Hispanics/Latinos are under-represented among lay ecclesial ministers relative to their proportion in the Catholic population overall.

Geographic Distribution of Lay Ecclesial Ministers

Lay ecclesial ministers comprise about one-fifth of the ecclesial workforce of Church personnel nationwide.[3] They are somewhat under-represented in the South, from Delaware through Texas, and in the Northeast, from Maine through Pennsylvania. All other regions of the country employ lay ecclesial ministers at a rate equal to or exceeding the national average. Upper Midwestern states such as Minnesota, North and South Dakota and Northwestern states such as Idaho, Montana, Oregon, and Washington have the highest concentrations of lay ecclesial ministers. Nearly one in three pastoral ministers in those regions are lay ecclesial ministers, a number of whom are entrusted with the leadership of parishes that have no resident pastor.

Map 9.1 illustrates the distribution of lay ecclesial ministers in dioceses across the United States. While their numbers are highest in areas with the greatest concentration of Catholic population, lay ecclesial ministers are active in most parishes around the country. Many other lay ecclesial ministers are also employed in dioceses, serving in roles such as chancellor, vicar of finance, and directors and staffs of diocesan offices such as religious education, worship, and lay formation.

Emerging Roles for Lay Ecclesial Ministers

Several new roles have emerged in the Church in the United States since the Second Vatican Council. The oldest is that of Director of Religious Education (DRE). The first DREs began emerging in parishes in the mid-

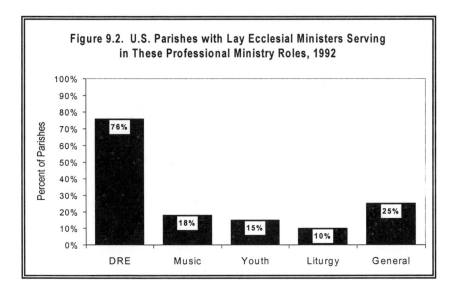

Figure 9.2. U.S. Parishes with Lay Ecclesial Ministers Serving in These Professional Ministry Roles, 1992

1960s – well before decreases in the numbers of priests and religious. By the mid-1980s many parishes had grown considerably in size as the Catholic population continued to grow but relatively few parishes were created. As a result of this and other factors, many parishes now had greater pastoral and liturgical needs, increasing supplies of ministry professionals – as well as the financial scale they needed to afford lay pastoral ministers, youth ministers, liturgy directors, music ministers, directors of social concerns, and other specialized positions. Figure 9.2 shows the distribution of lay ministry roles in parishes.[4]

Not surprisingly, parish size remains a crucial factor in determining need and budget for specialized parish staff positions, as the table below shows.

Table 9.3. Percent of Parishes with Specialized Parish Staff

	Very Large	Large	Mid-size	Small
Director of Religious Education	95%	90%	84%	71%
Parish Youth Minister	73	60	54	39

- More than nine in ten large parishes (those with more than 3,000 parishioners) have a parish Director of Religious Education (Coordinator or Associate for Religious Education are other titles sometimes used, ordinarily to reflect lesser levels of education). However, even mid-size (450 to 1,200 parishioners) and small (450 or fewer parishioners) parishes are more likely than not to have this specialized position.

- More than half of mid-size and larger parishes now have parish youth ministers. Nearly four in ten small parishes also have a parish youth minister. Altogether, nearly 12,000 serve as parish youth ministers today.

Diocesan Support for Lay Ecclesial Ministers

Diocesan involvement in lay ecclesial ministry is on the rise. In just the past five years dioceses are becoming increasingly involved in assisting with the recruiting, hiring, training, and support of lay ecclesial ministers, as Table 9.4 shows. Both parish ministers themselves and the pastors for whom they work support this trend. Parish ministers look for diocesan involvement in evaluating them, as well as in ministry training and support. Pastors see a need for more diocesan involvement in screening potential parish ministers, as well as certification and training.

Table 9.4. Diocesan Involvement in Lay Ecclesial Ministers' Placement
Percent of ministers reporting diocesan involvement

	1992	1997
Recruiting	9%	17%
Training	8	22
Screening	10	35
Certification	10	40
Commissioning	6	20
Evaluation	5	17
Policies, salary ranges, etc.	11	72
Continuing education	9	76
Included in diocesan events	8	83
Staff training and development	9	49

LAY ECCLESIAL MINISTRY FORMATION

Lay ministers on the whole are well educated, although their formal ministerial and theological education may have been unrelated to their actual ministry responsibilities. Four out of five have a college education and more than half have at least a master's degree. Lay persons tend to have somewhat lower levels of education than vowed religious in parish

Table 9.5. Educational Background of Parish Ministers

	Laity	Religious
High School or Less	6%	0%
Some College	20	1
College Graduate	16	8
Post-baccalaureate	17	8
Master's degree	36	77
Master of Divinity	3	4
Doctor of Ministry	<1	2
Ph.D. or S.T.D.	2	0

ministry. Table 9.5 compares the educational background of lay ecclesial ministers to whether they are vowed religious or lay.[5]

Trends in Lay Ministry Formation

There have been six nationwide surveys of formation programs designed to prepare lay Catholics for parish-level Church ministry. The Bishops' Committee on the Laity completed the first study in 1986, and other studies by CARA followed in 1994, 1996, 1997, and 1998. Information for the sixth study was collected by CARA in Fall 1999 with extensive follow-up in early 2000. As in the previous studies, an effort was made to limit the scope of the survey to full-length programs of at least two years' duration that provide for professional-level lay ministry training.

The role of the laity and their participation in the ministry of the Church have evolved considerably in the decades since the Second Vatican Council. At the same time, the number of formation programs to train lay people for professional Church ministry has increased, and many programs have expanded their scope. Since the first study of lay ministry formation in 1985-86, the number of programs has increased by over 50 percent, and the number of participants in these programs has grown almost three-fold.

A total of 331 active lay ministry formation programs were identified in 1999-2000. Current enrollment information was obtained from all but 48. These programs can be found in 151 dioceses, in each of the 50 states and the District of Columbia. Of the 283 programs that sent information, seven do not have students at this time but expect to begin enrollment in the near future.

The total number of participants in the other 276 programs that report current enrollments is 31,168, averaging 113 persons per program. Enrollments reported for the past two years are significantly higher than those reported in previous CARA studies, due in part to the continued growth in the number of such programs, as well as improved in data collection.

Table 9.6. Lay Ministry Formation Programs, 1985-2000				
Year	States	Dioceses	Programs	Enrollments
1985-86	43	110	206	10,500
1994-95	51	135	265	21,800
1996-97	49	145	281	20,281
1997-98	49	146	287	23,333
1998-99	51	150	296	29,137
1999-00	51	151	331	31,168

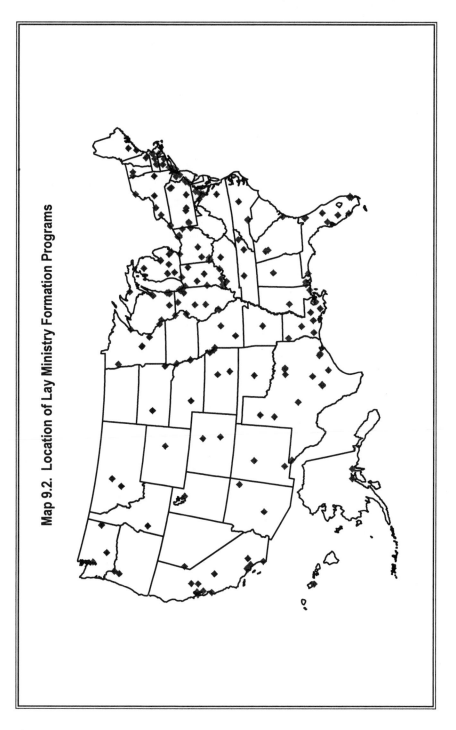

Map 9.2. Location of Lay Ministry Formation Programs

Program Profile

There are a number of different types of lay ministry formation programs. Most can be classified as either diocesan-based or academic-based. Currently, 189 programs are sponsored by a diocese or archdiocese and 96 programs are sponsored by a Catholic college or university. Of the diocesan-sponsored programs, 11 are affiliated with a seminary and 95 are affiliated with a college or university. Fifty-eight of the programs that are both diocesan-sponsored and college or university-affiliated are sites of either the Loyola Institute for Ministry Extension, ("LIMEX" with 50 programs) or the Certificate of Advanced Studies in Pastoral Life and Administration, ("CAS" with eight programs), both based at Loyola University in New Orleans. In addition to academic and diocesan based programs, independent Catholic organizations sponsor ten other programs. Six of these independent programs are related to the Education for Parish Service (EPS), based at Trinity College in Washington, D.C. Another 20 independent programs are sponsored by Catholic hospitals to train ministers in clinical pastoral education (CPE).

Academic-based programs usually offer formal academic degrees, but many also offer certificates. Similarly, diocesan-based programs affiliated with a seminary, college, or university generally offer opportunities for both academic degrees and certificates. Programs that are exclusively diocesan-sponsored typically offer non-degree certificates only.

Most of the degree-granting programs offer graduate degrees, although a few grant associate's or baccalaureate degrees. The most commonly offered graduate degrees in degree-granting lay ministry programs are the M.A. in Pastoral Studies or Pastoral Ministry (65 programs), the M.A. in Theology or Theological Studies (52 programs), and the M.A. in Religious Education (43 programs). In addition, nine programs grant doctoral degrees—three grant the Ph.D., three the D.Min., and three the S.T.D., (Doctor of Sacred Theology, conferred with the authorization of the Holy See).

Nearly all (98 percent) of lay ministry programs grant certificates; 40 percent grant *only* certificates. The most common certificate programs are in Pastoral Ministry (87 programs), Catechetics (59 programs), Youth Ministry (50 programs), Religious Education (49 programs), and Liturgy (44 programs).

Lay ministry formation programs are conducted in a variety of languages. Of the 276 programs reporting the language of instruction, 222 use only English, 43 use both English and Spanish, and 11 use Spanish only. In addition, one program uses English, Spanish, and American Sign Language; another uses English, Spanish, and Portuguese; two more use

English and American Sign Language; and a fourth uses English and Navajo.

Profile of Lay Ministry Program Participants

Women outnumber men among program participants by a ratio of nearly two to one. Only small percentages are members of the clergy or belong to religious communities. Figure 9.3 depicts the percentages of participants who are lay women, lay men, women religious, men religious, priests, and deacons. Approximately three percent of enrollments are non-Catholic.

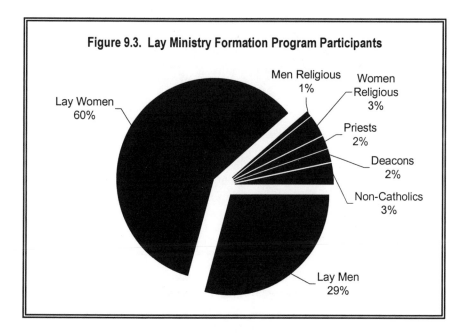

Figure 9.3. Lay Ministry Formation Program Participants

Age Distribution of Lay Ministry Program Participants

About one in four students in lay ministry formation programs is under 40. More than 60 percent are between 40 and 60. Figure 9.4 presents the complete age distribution. Nearly as many lay ministry program participants are under age 30 (eight percent) as are 60 and above (11 percent). Thus, lay ministry program participants vary in terms of age much more than deacon formation candidates.

Racial and Ethnic Background of Lay Ministry Program Participants

Although nearly three-fourths of participants in lay ministry formation programs are white, Hispanic/Latinos also comprise a sizeable group of lay

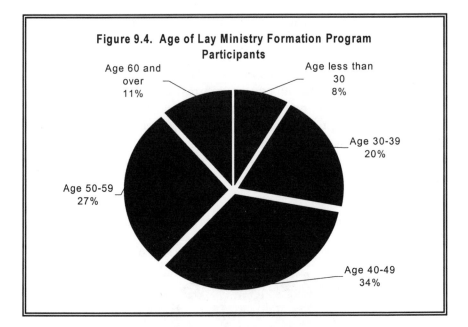

Figure 9.4. Age of Lay Ministry Formation Program Participants

- Age 60 and over 11%
- Age less than 30 8%
- Age 30-39 20%
- Age 50-59 27%
- Age 40-49 34%

ministry enrollments. The numbers of blacks, Asians, and Native Americans are considerably lower, but generally comparable with their overall presence in the Catholic population. These latter three groups form only six percent of lay ministry enrollments, as shown in figure 9.5.

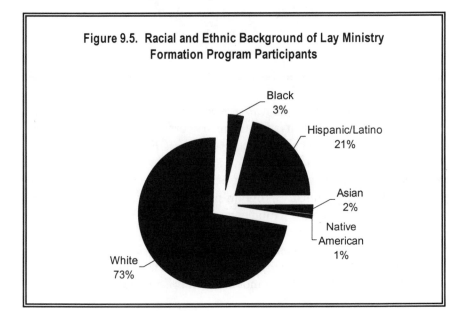

Figure 9.5. Racial and Ethnic Background of Lay Ministry Formation Program Participants

- Black 3%
- Hispanic/Latino 21%
- Asian 2%
- Native American 1%
- White 73%

CONCLUSION

The vision of the Second Vatican Council was oriented toward creating an awareness that the path to holiness is open to all. Whereas the Council of Trent (1545-1563) had clarified the special order of the priesthood, and the separate status and rank that ordination implied, the Second Vatican Council emphasized that the call to minister is not restricted to priests and religious. The Council's 1965 decree *Apostolicam Actuositatem* (On the Apostolate of the Laity), reads, "in the Church there is a diversity of ministry, but unity of mission." A generation later, there are now a variety of ministries that are needed by the Church and to which lay people are increasingly responding. As that decree and Church realities attest, there is a wide variety of ministries required by the contemporary Catholic Church to which lay people can contribute.

Today, as called for at the Second Vatican Council, the Church now enjoys a new time of diversity in ministry. The Church benefits from the gifts of the ordained – priests and deacons – and from those of lay people – religious women and men, volunteers and paid professionals, and all those Catholics living their faith in the world. In all there is a certain unity of mission as they work together to build the Church.

The sacramental vision of Catholicism recognizes and respects each of the different roles and ministries. Some have a specific sacramental character conferred by the sacrament of orders, but all share in common the call they received in baptism.

The unique role of the priest focuses on the celebration of the sacraments and presiding at Eucharist as leader of the assembly. The role of the deacon is to assist the priest in sacramental life, and, consistent with the mission of service, to act on behalf of those in need in the local parish community and elsewhere. Religious women and men live out their unique charism in ministry to the community in many different ways. The lay ecclesial minister brings specialized training in areas such as catechesis, youth, music, social services, education, charitable activity, social justice advocacy, and others.

In continuity with their history and traditions, and through their institutions, ministers, and own participation, Catholics have built an enormous base from which they can respond to the challenges of the twenty-first century. As the Catholic Church in the United States looks ahead to the future, it can count on a diverse and growing Catholic population, a rich institutional life, and a diverse pastoral workforce. At the heart of all these developments, however, is the simple message expressed in the Latin title of the Vatican II document *On the Church in the Modern World*: *Gaudium et Spes*, Hope and Joy.[6]

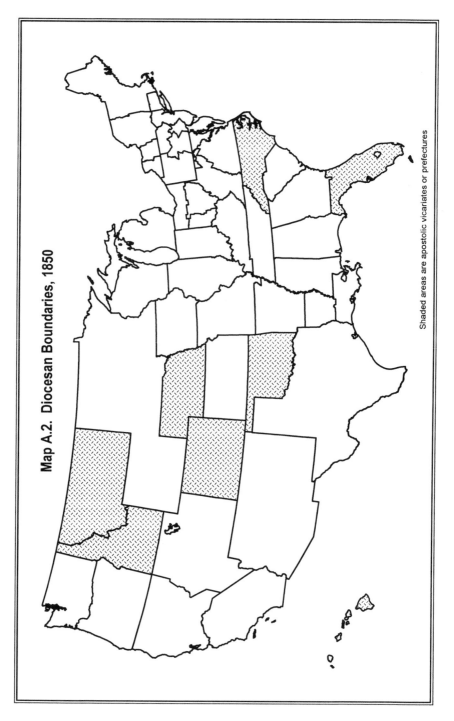

Map A.2. Diocesan Boundaries, 1850

Shaded areas are apostolic vicariates or prefectures

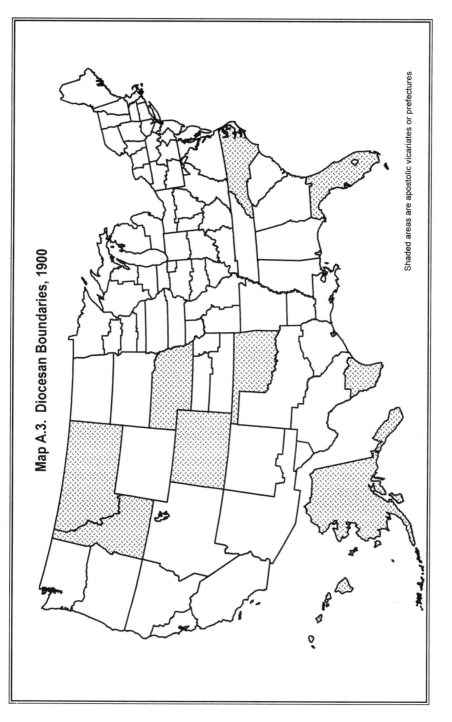

Map A.3. Diocesan Boundaries, 1900

Shaded areas are apostolic vicariates or prefectures

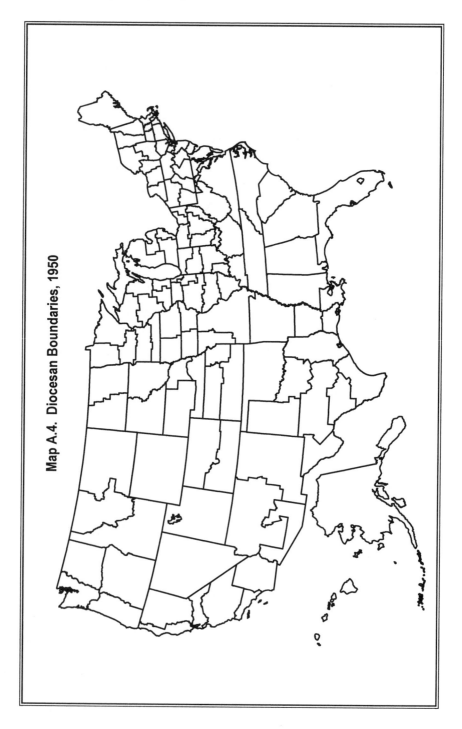

Map A.4. Diocesan Boundaries, 1950

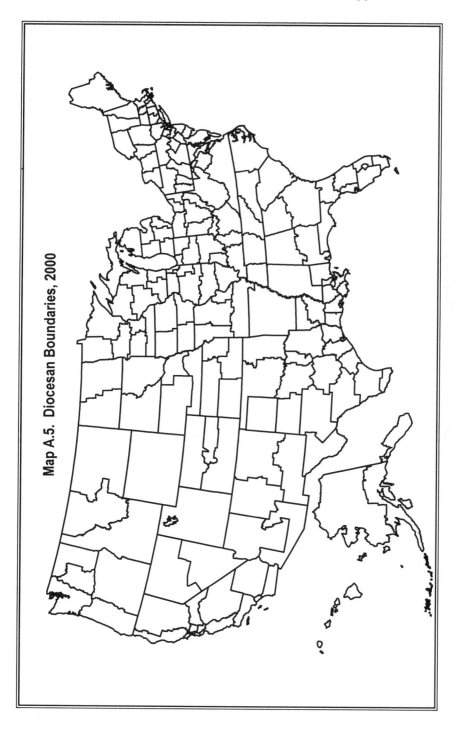

Map A.5. Diocesan Boundaries, 2000

Table A.2. Dioceses by Population, with Percent Catholic

Diocese	Catholics	Population	Percent
Archdiocese of Los Angeles	4,080,793	10,652,600	38%
Archdiocese of New York	2,371,355	5,254,300	45%
Archdiocese of Chicago	2,358,000	5,682,000	41%
Archdiocese of Boston	2,042,688	3,761,400	54%
Diocese of Brooklyn	1,625,547	4,216,060	39%
Archdiocese of Detroit	1,453,756	4,266,650	34%
Archdiocese of Philadelphia	1,411,256	3,706,022	38%
Diocese of Rockville Centre	1,359,432	2,907,955	47%
Archdiocese of Newark	1,319,558	2,651,785	50%
Diocese of Galveston-Houston	906,330	4,396,876	21%
Diocese of Cleveland	827,971	2,822,180	29%
Diocese of San Bernardino	821,443	3,042,385	27%
Archdiocese of Miami	787,672	3,597,277	22%
Diocese of San Diego	776,093	2,866,727	27%
Diocese of Brownsville	774,056	906,945	85%
Archdiocese of Hartford	757,793	1,806,705	42%
Diocese of Pittsburgh	755,459	1,995,320	38%
Archdiocese of St. Paul and Minneapolis	752,325	2,757,989	27%
Diocese of Buffalo	741,506	1,587,808	47%
Diocese of Trenton	703,531	1,763,249	40%
Archdiocese of Milwaukee	695,934	2,197,939	32%
Archdiocese of San Antonio	673,026	1,890,760	36%
Diocese of Providence	629,891	987,429	64%
Diocese of Orange	615,041	2,674,091	23%
Diocese of El Paso	597,275	784,511	76%
Diocese of Dallas	555,172	2,971,699	19%
Archdiocese of St. Louis	555,000	2,064,548	27%
Archdiocese of Cincinnati	547,000	2,901,082	19%
Diocese of Joliet	538,078	1,494,978	36%
Archdiocese of Washington	510,000	2,413,700	21%
Archdiocese of Seattle	508,900	4,425,100	12%
Diocese of Oakland	496,122	2,255,100	22%
Diocese of Metuchen	495,322	1,194,578	41%
Archdiocese of Baltimore	484,287	2,849,409	17%
Archdiocese of New Orleans	482,373	1,332,771	36%
Diocese of Sacramento	454,000	2,873,646	16%
Diocese of Phoenix	423,525	3,113,775	14%
Archdiocese of San Francisco	422,000	1,700,000	25%
Diocese of Camden	418,713	1,291,117	32%
Diocese of Albany	403,403	1,340,388	30%
Diocese of Paterson	403,207	1,080,261	37%
Diocese of San Jose	400,226	1,609,037	25%

Diocese	Catholics	Population	Percent
Diocese of Las Vegas	390,000	1,300,000	30%
Diocese of Green Bay	388,150	898,050	43%
Diocese of Syracuse	372,665	1,223,591	30%
Diocese of Corpus Christi	363,000	863,242	42%
Diocese of Scranton	362,546	1,054,814	34%
Diocese of Bridgeport	360,918	833,315	43%
Diocese of St. Petersburg	358,951	2,393,006	15%
Diocese of Austin	350,000	1,915,392	18%
Diocese of Fresno	349,663	2,263,150	15%
Archdiocese of Denver	346,144	2,644,004	13%
Diocese of Fall River	341,482	721,500	47%
Diocese of Rochester	337,613	1,479,727	23%
Diocese of Lafayette in Louisiana	336,746	559,055	60%
Diocese of Arlington	336,123	2,228,575	15%
Diocese of Tucson	335,520	1,307,412	26%
Diocese of Manchester	330,513	1,173,000	28%
Diocese of Orlando	323,766	3,094,540	10%
Diocese of Rockford	323,109	1,228,630	26%
Diocese of Toledo	322,938	1,402,733	23%
Archdiocese of Atlanta	311,000	4,945,355	6%
Diocese of Worcester	302,000	790,705	38%
Archdiocese of Portland in Oregon	289,951	2,799,200	10%
Diocese of Springfield in Massachusetts	288,967	800,500	36%
Diocese of Madison	260,817	885,562	29%
Diocese of Allentown	259,847	1,084,189	24%
Archdiocese of Santa Fe	257,258	1,044,376	25%
Diocese of Youngstown	256,802	1,222,866	21%
Diocese of Honolulu	236,688	1,186,602	20%
Diocese of Harrisburg	234,831	1,940,954	12%
Diocese of Peoria	232,366	1,447,418	16%
Diocese of Erie	229,659	874,900	26%
Diocese of Portland in Maine	227,183	1,227,927	19%
Diocese of Palm Beach	224,364	1,445,543	16%
Diocese of Norwich	224,259	638,244	35%
Diocese of La Crosse	219,358	824,206	27%
Archdiocese of Dubuque	218,108	923,000	24%
Archdiocese of Indianapolis	217,886	2,201,503	10%
Archdiocese of Omaha	214,574	822,892	26%
Diocese of Lansing	210,878	1,695,979	12%
Diocese of Baton Rouge	207,511	809,065	26%
Diocese of Fort Worth	207,490	2,372,666	9%
Diocese of Columbus	193,955	2,243,099	9%
Diocese of Richmond	191,051	4,507,819	4%
Archdiocese of Kansas City in Kansas	190,418	952,000	20%
Diocese of Greensburg	187,166	679,421	28%

Dioceses by Population, with Percent Catholic, cont.

Diocese	Catholics	Population	Percent
Diocese of Gary	184,430	759,673	24%
Diocese of Monterey	179,110	895,550	20%
Archdiocese of Louisville	178,420	1,139,022	16%
Diocese of Venice	175,216	1,421,844	12%
Diocese of Wilmington	173,702	1,108,890	16%
Diocese of Stockton	171,622	1,069,310	16%
Diocese of Springfield in Illinois	163,713	1,106,124	15%
Diocese of Kansas City-St. Joseph	156,870	1,299,555	12%
Diocese of Fort Wayne-South Bend	156,621	1,156,129	14%
Diocese of Grand Rapids	153,601	1,167,900	13%
Diocese of Winona	148,445	528,303	28%
Diocese of St. Cloud	148,243	474,546	31%
Diocese of Burlington	147,840	598,000	25%
Diocese of Santa Rosa	141,792	745,138	19%
Diocese of Raleigh	141,515	3,646,035	4%
Diocese of Saginaw	139,876	685,532	20%
Diocese of Las Cruces	136,499	474,499	29%
Diocese of Ogdensburg	136,090	430,422	32%
Diocese of St. Augustine	131,478	1,570,181	8%
Diocese of Houma-Thibodaux	130,274	202,000	64%
Diocese of Sioux Falls	122,950	503,000	24%
Diocese of Boise	122,640	1,250,000	10%
Diocese of Charleston	121,637	3,760,000	3%
Diocese of Charlotte	119,160	3,882,756	3%
Diocese of Altoona-Johnstown	115,210	647,357	18%
Diocese of Kalamazoo	114,632	912,044	13%
Diocese of Wichita	109,859	916,007	12%
Diocese of Belleville	109,233	853,645	13%
Diocese of Victoria	108,562	255,276	43%
Diocese of Pueblo	107,723	600,000	18%
Diocese of Davenport	106,460	726,646	15%
Diocese of Des Moines	99,224	671,091	15%
Diocese of Fargo	98,915	391,000	25%
Diocese of Salt Lake City	98,800	2,591,045	4%
Diocese of Lafayette in Indiana	97,662	1,115,156	9%
Diocese of Wheeling-Charleston	97,232	1,815,787	5%
Archdiocese of Oklahoma City	92,391	2,209,100	4%
Diocese of Evansville	89,973	482,447	19%
Diocese of Jefferson City	89,730	799,266	11%
Diocese of Little Rock	89,091	2,522,813	4%
Diocese of Superior	88,288	394,960	22%
Diocese of Lincoln	88,056	516,662	17%
Diocese of Beaumont	87,604	577,664	15%

Diocese	Catholics	Population	Percent
Diocese of Covington	85,202	401,127	21%
Diocese of Lake Charles	84,908	259,425	33%
Diocese of Sioux City	83,449	472,957	18%
Diocese of San Angelo	82,008	715,375	11%
Diocese of Duluth	81,560	417,125	20%
Diocese of Colorado Springs	81,515	702,808	12%
Diocese of Spokane	78,432	721,646	11%
Diocese of Savannah	74,800	2,465,277	3%
Diocese of Marquette	72,552	319,700	23%
Diocese of Birmingham	71,958	2,644,644	3%
Diocese of New Ulm	69,840	278,780	25%
Diocese of Yakima	66,819	461,600	14%
Diocese of Bismarck	66,763	253,552	26%
Diocese of Biloxi	66,507	726,476	9%
Diocese of Helena	66,500	424,372	16%
Archdiocese of Mobile	66,013	1,452,506	5%
Diocese of Pensacola-Tallahassee	65,904	1,274,850	5%
Diocese of Reno	64,870	527,778	12%
Diocese of Nashville	63,363	1,824,375	3%
Diocese of Memphis	60,804	1,438,524	4% ᵃ
Diocese of Tulsa	57,800	1,478,542	4% ↗
Diocese of Springfield-Cape Girardeau	57,439	1,155,600	5%
Diocese of Lubbock	55,781	410,180	14%
Diocese of Great Falls-Billings	55,117	392,900	14%
Diocese of Grand Island	53,967	290,429	19%
Diocese of Tyler	52,362	1,211,878	4%
Diocese of Salina	51,779	321,132	16%
Diocese of Owensboro	51,702	778,235	7%
Diocese of Cheyenne	49,800	484,010	10%
Diocese of Alexandria	48,050	401,211	12%
Diocese of Amarillo	46,356	393,822	12%
Diocese of Jackson	45,408	1,980,025	2%
Diocese of Gallup	44,480	379,555	12%
Diocese of Knoxville	43,765	2,012,885	2%
Diocese of Dodge City	42,566	212,332	20%
Diocese of Crookston	42,122	236,100	18%
Diocese of Lexington	41,977	1,444,148	3%
Diocese of Steubenville	41,452	520,177	8%
Diocese of Shreveport	37,877	770,129	5%
Diocese of Rapid City	35,605	211,591	17%
Diocese of Baker	35,588	417,800	9%
Archdiocese of Anchorage	29,307	389,401	8%
Diocese of Fairbanks	16,846	141,759	12%
Diocese of Juneau	6,043	74,285	8%

Table A.3. Dioceses by Number of Catholic Elementary and High Schools

Diocese or Eparchy	Schools	Students	Parishes
Archdiocese of Chicago	318	130,570	378
Archdiocese of New York	293	103,387	413
Archdiocese of Los Angeles	279	99,184	287
Archdiocese of Philadelphia	278	120,180	287
>Archdiocese of St. Louis	185	58,898	227
Archdiocese of Newark	181	60,365	236
Diocese of Brooklyn	178	72,641	218
Archdiocese of Boston	165	54,637	382
Archdiocese of Detroit	165	52,832	306
Diocese of Cleveland	163	66,286	235
Archdiocese of Milwaukee	159	40,848	254
Archdiocese of Cincinnati	134	57,137	235
Diocese of Pittsburgh	121	32,621	218
Diocese of Buffalo	111	29,759	265
Archdiocese of New Orleans	104	50,649	146
Archdiocese of Washington	104	38,190	139
Archdiocese of St. Paul and Minneapolis	100	35,243	222
Diocese of Toledo	100	29,062	163
Archdiocese of Baltimore	95	35,736	155
Diocese of La Crosse	85	12,262	173
Diocese of Green Bay	84	15,429	199
Archdiocese of Hartford	82	24,048	220
Archdiocese of Omaha	80	22,194	139
Archdiocese of San Francisco	78	28,904	93
Diocese of Rockville Centre	75	41,314	134
Diocese of Trenton	72	29,303	127
Archdiocese of Miami	71	34,827	108
Archdiocese of Indianapolis	71	24,889	138
Diocese of Paterson	71	20,966	111
Archdiocese of Louisville	69	25,240	113
Diocese of Allentown	65	18,583	153
Diocese of Joliet	64	25,419	120
Archdiocese of Seattle	64	21,692	138
Diocese of Rochester	63	17,258	161
Diocese of Providence	62	19,820	158
Diocese of Camden	61	21,383	126
Diocese of Oakland	61	21,370	89
Diocese of Scranton	61	16,699	200
Diocese of Springfield in Illinois	61	14,733	165

Diocese or Eparchy	Schools	Students	Parishes
Diocese of Galveston-Houston	59	17,368	151
Diocese of Columbus	57	19,051	107
Diocese of Peoria	54	15,017	165
Diocese of Sacramento	53	17,043	98
Archdiocese of San Antonio	51	17,253	144
Diocese of Harrisburg	51	15,427	89
Diocese of Youngstown	51	14,426	116
Archdiocese of Portland in Oregon	51	14,338	125
Diocese of Erie	51	13,847	127
Diocese of Metuchen	50	18,028	108
Archdiocese of Kansas City in Kansas	50	15,079	119
Diocese of Dallas	49	18,545	65
Diocese of San Diego	49	16,927	98
Diocese of Rockford	49	16,498	105
Diocese of St. Petersburg	49	14,132	73
Diocese of Syracuse	49	12,667	172
Diocese of Lansing	47	13,262	95
Diocese of Albany	47	12,131	186
Diocese of Madison	47	8,226	137
Diocese of Orange	44	19,629	54
Diocese of Fort Wayne-South Bend	44	14,094	87
Diocese of Bridgeport	43	13,831	88
Archdiocese of Denver	42	14,135	112
Diocese of Grand Rapids	42	9,167	90
Diocese of Kansas City-St. Joseph	41	16,560	84
Diocese of Lafayette in Louisiana	41	14,984	121
Diocese of Manchester	41	10,299	131
Diocese of Arlington	40	16,827	63
Diocese of Covington	40	11,788	48
Diocese of Belleville	40	9,111	127
Diocese of Jefferson City	39	7,169	95
Diocese of Wilmington	37	15,358	55
Diocese of San Bernardino	37	9,490	97
Diocese of Little Rock	37	8,616	90
Diocese of Springfield in Massachusetts	36	9,550	130
Diocese of Wichita	36	9,480	92
Diocese of Sioux City	36	8,599	116
Diocese of San Jose	35	16,238	48
Diocese of Orlando	35	14,850	70
Diocese of Richmond	35	10,364	142
Diocese of Wheeling-Charleston	35	7,175	113

Dioceses by Number of Catholic Elementary and High Schools, cont.

Diocese or Eparchy	Schools	Students	Parishes
Diocese of St. Cloud	35	7,030	140
Diocese of Baton Rouge	34	16,896	70
Diocese of Honolulu	34	11,407	66
Diocese of Gary	34	9,698	77
Diocese of Altoona-Johnstown	33	6,104	112
Diocese of Saginaw	33	6,076	110
Diocese of Worcester	32	10,680	126
Diocese of Winona	32	6,654	118
Diocese of Lincoln	30	7,577	134
Diocese of Greensburg	30	6,600	107
Diocese of Fall River	29	8,675	111
Diocese of Evansville	29	7,908	70
Diocese of Phoenix	28	11,775	86
Diocese of Norwich	28	6,598	78
Diocese of Tucson	27	7,236	64
Diocese of Davenport	27	5,792	89
Diocese of Charleston	26	7,839	85
Diocese of Ogdensburg	26	4,934	120
Diocese of Springfield-Cape Girardeau	26	4,617	64
Diocese of Fresno	25	6,890	84
Diocese of Birmingham	25	6,883	54
Diocese of Corpus Christi	25	5,481	84
Diocese of Sioux Falls	25	5,268	156
Diocese of Kalamazoo	25	4,886	46
Archdiocese of Mobile	24	7,571	76
Diocese of St. Augustine	23	9,256	50
Diocese of Gaylord	23	3,983	81
Diocese of Owensboro	22	5,259	79
Diocese of Portland in Maine	22	5,181	138
Diocese of Lafayette in Indiana	22	4,654	62
Diocese of New Ulm	22	3,960	81
Archdiocese of Oklahoma City	21	5,038	72
Diocese of Fort Worth	20	8,029	87
Diocese of Savannah	20	6,518	53
Diocese of Santa Rosa	20	5,069	43
Diocese of Austin	20	4,169	95
Diocese of Jackson	20	4,023	74
Diocese of Palm Beach	19	7,199	46
Diocese of Memphis	19	6,294	42
Diocese of Biloxi	19	5,215	44

Diocese or Eparchy	Schools	Students	Parishes
Diocese of Spokane	19	4,595	78
Diocese of Raleigh	18	5,628	70
Diocese of Monterey	18	5,424	46
Diocese of Lexington	18	4,358	60
Diocese of Steubenville	18	3,547	73
Diocese of Superior	18	2,887	114
Diocese of Charlotte	17	7,068	67
Diocese of Des Moines	17	6,164	87
Archdiocese of Santa Fe	17	5,754	91
Diocese of Nashville	17	5,322	50
Diocese of Bismarck	17	3,145	62
Diocese of Salina	17	2,642	92
Diocese of Victoria	16	3,154	50
Archdiocese of Atlanta	15	6,855	69
Diocese of El Paso	15	5,384	58
Diocese of Burlington	15	3,384	94
Diocese of Stockton	14	4,748	32
Diocese of Tulsa	14	4,728	81
Diocese of Boise	14	3,249	58
Diocese of Great Falls-Billings	14	2,971	52
Diocese of Houma-Thibodaux	13	6,331	40
Diocese of Fargo	13	2,415	159
Diocese of Gallup	13	1,954	58
Diocese of Duluth	13	1,905	94
Diocese of Venice	12	5,084	50
Diocese of Salt Lake City	12	4,188	43
Diocese of Alexandria	12	3,378	48
Diocese of Shreveport	11	2,958	31
Diocese of Grand Island	11	1,875	43
Diocese of Knoxville	10	3,551	43
Diocese of Pensacola-Tallahassee	10	3,152	54
Diocese of Marquette	10	1,705	74
Diocese of Crookston	10	1,375	71
Diocese of Dodge City	10	1,150	51
Diocese of Lake Charles	9	3,623	36
Diocese of Brownsville	9	3,411	63
Diocese of Yakima	9	2,020	41
Diocese of Amarillo	9	1,086	35
Diocese of Las Vegas	7	3,431	24
Diocese of Beaumont	7	2,466	44
Diocese of Cheyenne	7	1,128	36

Dioceses by Number of Catholic Elementary and High Schools, cont.

Diocese or Eparchy	Schools	Students	Parishes
Diocese of Pueblo	6	1,351	53
Diocese of Helena	6	1,165	58
Diocese of Reno	5	1,695	28
Diocese of Tyler	5	1,064	35
Diocese of Colorado Springs	4	1,348	31
Diocese of Rapid City	4	1,297	95
Exarchy for Armenian Catholics	4	1,016	7
Diocese of Las Cruces	4	542	44
Archdiocese of Anchorage	4	529	19
Diocese of San Angelo	3	850	49
Diocese of Baker	3	586	35
Archeparchy of Pittsburgh (Byzantine)	3	533	85
Eparchy of Passaic (Byzantine)	3	449	97
Diocese of Fairbanks	2	476	41
Diocese of Lubbock	2	429	36
Eparchy of Parma (Byzantine)	2	325	38
Eparchy of St. Josaphat in Parma (Ukrainian)	2	272	38
Diocese of Juneau	1	85	10
Eparchy of Newton (Melkite-Greek)	0	0	35
Eparchy of St. Maron, Brooklyn (Maronite)	0	0	34
Eparchy of Our Lady of Lebanon (Maronite)	0	0	27
Eparchy of Van Nuys (Byzantine)	0	0	16
Eparchy of St. George's in Canton (Romanian)	0	0	15
Eparchy of St. Thomas the Apostle (Chaldean)	0	0	12
Eparchy of Our Lady of Deliverance (Syrian)	0	0	8

Table A.4. Theologates by Date Founded, with 1999-2000 Enrollments

Theologate	Founded	Enrollment
St. Mary's Seminary and University, Baltimore, MD	1791	90
Mt. St. Mary Seminary, Emmitsburg, MD	1808	168
Athenaeum of Ohio, Mt. St. Mary Seminary of the West, Cincinnati, OH	1829	37
St. Charles Borromeo Seminary, Wynnewood, PA	1832	81
Dominican House of Studies, Washington, DC	1834	41
Moreau Seminary, University of Notre Dame, Notre Dame, IN	1842	34
St. Francis Seminary, Saint Francis, WI	1845	18
St. Vincent Seminary, Latrobe, PA	1846	97
St. Mary Seminary, Wickliffe, OH	1848	30

Theologate	Founded	Enrollment
Dominican School of Philosophy and Theology, Berkeley, CA	1851	39
Immaculate Conception Seminary, South Orange, NJ	1856	132
St. John's School of Theology, Collegeville, MN	1857	10
American College of Louvain, Leuven, Belgium	1857	22
Christ the King Seminary, East Aurora, NY	1857	25
North American College, Rome, Italy	1859	184
St. Meinrad School of Theology, St. Meinrad, IN	1861	84
St. John's Seminary School of Theology, Brighton, MA	1884	78
SS. Cyril and Methodius Seminary, Orchard Lake, MI	1885	39
Pontifical College Josephinum, Columbus, OH	1888	78
Theological College/School of Religious Studies, The Catholic University, Washington, DC	1889	73
Mt. Angel Seminary, Saint Benedict, OR	1889	90
Kenrick School of Theology, Saint Louis, MO	1893	70
St. Paul Seminary School of Divinity, Saint Paul, MN	1894	80
St. Joseph's Seminary, Yonkers, NY	1896	55
St. Patrick's Seminary, Menlo Park, CA	1898	85
St. Mary's Seminary, Houston, TX	1901	56
Oblate School of Theology, San Antonio, TX	1903	69
Mundelein Seminary, University of St. Mary of the Lake, Mundelein, IL	1921	191
Weston Jesuit School of Theology, Cambridge, MA	1922	82
Notre Dame Seminary, New Orleans, LA	1923	150
Aquinas Institute of Theology, Saint Louis, MO	1925	34
Seminary of the Immaculate Conception, Huntington, NY	1930	41
Sacred Heart School of Theology, Hales Corners, WI	1933	102
Jesuit School of Theology, Berkeley, CA	1934	40
St. Anthony Seminary, El Paso, TX	1936	43
St. John's Seminary, Camarillo, CA	1939	78
SS. Cyril & Methodius Seminary, Pittsburgh, PA (Byzantine Catholic)	1950	9
Holy Apostles College and Seminary, Cromwell, CT	1956	70
St. Vincent De Paul Regional Seminary, Boynton Beach, FL	1961	77
Pope John XXIII National Seminary, Weston, MA	1964	70
Washington Theological Union, Washington, DC	1968	107
Catholic Theological Union, Chicago, IL	1968	145
Franciscan School of Theology, Berkeley, CA	1968	8
Sacred Heart Major Seminary, Detroit, MI	1988	48
Our Lady of Guadalupe Seminary, Elmhurst, PA	1993	60
St. John Vianney Theological Seminary, Denver, CO	1999	45

Table A.5. Free-standing College Seminaries by Date Founded, with 1999-2000 Enrollments

College Seminary	Founded	Enrollment
St. Charles Borromeo Seminary College, Wynnewood, PA	1832	84
Conception Seminary College, Conception, MO	1886	89
Josephinum College of Liberal Arts, Columbus, OH	1888	46
Mt. Angel Seminary College, Saint Benedict, OR	1889	89
St. Joseph Seminary College, Saint Benedict, LA	1891	74
Divine Word College Seminary, Epworth, IA	1912	86
Sacred Heart Major Seminary-College, Detroit, MI	1919	30
Wadhams Hall Seminary-College, Ogdensburg, NY	1924	22
St. Basil College, Stamford, CT	1939	58
Holy Apostles Seminary, Cromwell, CT	1956	10
St. John's Seminary College, Camarillo, CA	1961	88
Legionaries of Christ College Novitiate, Cheshire, CT	1965	130
St. John's Seminary College of Liberal Arts, Brighton, MA	1970	34
St. John Vianney College and Seminary, Miami, FL	1979	55
St. Gregory the Great Seminary, Seward, NE	1997	21

Table A.6. Collaborative College Seminaries by Date Founded, with 1999-2000 Enrollments

College	Founded	Enrollment
St. Pius X Seminary, Dubuque, IA	1838	9
College Seminary of the Immaculate Conception, South Orange, NJ	1861	21
St. Ambrose College Seminary, Davenport, IA	1882	4
St. Thomas Seminary, Bloomfield, CT	1897	6
Cardinal Glennon College, Saint Louis, MO	1931	35
Seminary of Our Lady of Providence, Providence, RI	1941	9
St. Francis Seminary, San Diego, CA	1941	22
St. Mark Seminary, Erie, PA	1946	13
Immaculate Heart of Mary Seminary, Winona, MN	1948	54
SS. Cyril & Methodius Seminary, Pittsburgh, PA (Byzantine Catholic)	1950	5
Borromeo Seminary, Wickliffe, OH	1954	35
Moreau Seminary, University of Notre Dame, Notre Dame, IN	1957	26
Bishop White Seminary, Spokane, WA	1958	5
Borromeo Pre-Seminary Program, Helena, MT	1960	7
St. Joseph College Seminary, Chicago, IL	1961	51

College	Founded	Enrollment
St. Pius X College Seminary, Dalton, PA	1962	16
St. Paul College Seminary, Pittsburgh, PA	1966	10
Holy Trinity College Seminary, Irving, TX	1967	38
St. John Vianney Seminary, Saint Paul, MN	1968	84
St. John Neumann College Seminary, Riverdale-on-Hudson, NY	1977	43
Franciscan University of Steubenville, Steubenville, OH	1985	80
Cathedral Seminary Residence of the Immaculate Conception, Douglaston, NY	1988	25
St. John Fisher Seminary Residence, Stamford, CT	1989	12
St. Francis Seminary College Program, Milwaukee, WI	1997	7

Table A.7. High School Seminaries by Date Founded, with 1999-2000 Enrollments

Freestanding High Schools	Founded	Enrollment
St. Lawrence Seminary, Mount Calvary, WI	1856	222
Cathedral Preparatory Seminary, Elmhurst, NY	1914	157
Immaculate Conception Apostolic School, Center Harbor, NH	1982	77
Archbishop Quigley Preparatory Seminary, Chicago, IL	1990	214
Collaborative High Schools	**Founded**	**Enrollment**
Cathedral Preparatory Seminary, Yonkers, NY	1903	20
St. Thomas Aquinas Preparatory Seminary, Hannibal, MO	1957	31
Cardinal Muench Seminary, Fargo, ND	1962	3
Holy Cross Seminary House of Formation, La Crosse, WI	1995	8

Table A.8. Diaconate Formation Programs by Date Founded, with 1999-2000 Enrollments

Diocese or Eparchy	Founded	Enrollment
Archdiocese of Washington	1967	27
Diocese of Charleston	1968	34
Diocese of Phoenix	1969	15
Diocese of Cleveland	1969	31
Diocese of San Diego	1969	20
Archdiocese of Hartford	1969	50

Diaconate Formation Programs by Date Founded and Enrollment, cont.

Diocese or Eparchy	Founded	Enrollment
Diocese of Des Moines	1970	13
Archdiocese of Detroit	1970	17
Archdiocese of Baltimore	1970	8
Archdiocese of Chicago	1970	98
Archdiocese of Chicago	1970	20
Diocese of Galveston-Houston	1970	71
Diocese of Green Bay	1970	38
Diocese of Fairbanks	1970	8
Diocese of Gallup	1970	12
Archdiocese of Cincinnati	1971	14
Archdiocese of San Antonio	1971	58
Archdiocese of New York	1971	48
Archdiocese of Omaha	1971	10
Archdiocese of Omaha	1971	36
Eparchy of Newton (Melkite-Greek)	1971	13
Diocese of Dallas	1971	36
Diocese of Kansas City-St. Joseph	1971	9
Archdiocese of Denver	1972	61
Diocese of Toledo	1972	5
Archdiocese of New Orleans	1972	40
Diocese of Tucson	1972	30
Archdiocese of Los Angeles	1972	93
Diocese of Rockford	1972	23
Diocese of Evansville	1973	N/A
Diocese of Fairbanks	1973	4
Diocese of Paterson	1973	22
Archdiocese of Boston	1973	41
Archdiocese of Milwaukee	1973	18
Archdiocese of Newark	1973	54
Archdiocese of St. Paul and Minneapolis	1973	35
Diocese of Providence	1974	15
Diocese of Trenton	1974	38
Diocese of Peoria	1974	31
Diocese of Buffalo	1974	27
Archdiocese of Louisville	1974	6
Diocese of Camden	1974	27
Archdiocese of St. Louis	1975	10
Archdiocese of Atlanta	1975	44
Diocese of Joliet	1975	51
Diocese of St. Cloud	1975	13
Diocese of Lafayette in Louisiana	1975	25
Diocese of Bridgeport	1975	23
Diocese of Youngstown	1975	7

Diocese or Eparchy	Founded	Enrollment
Diocese of Jefferson City	1975	16
Diocese of Corpus Christi	1975	17
Diocese of Tulsa	1975	8
Diocese of Rapid City	1975	2
Diocese of Amarillo	1975	9
Diocese of Syracuse	1975	12
Archdiocese of Dubuque	1976	13
Diocese of Biloxi	1976	8
Diocese of Savannah	1976	24
Diocese of Fall River	1976	19
Diocese of Worcester	1976	24
Diocese of Duluth	1976	9
Diocese of Brooklyn	1976	36
Diocese of Burlington	1976	0
Diocese of Albany	1976	9
Diocese of Rockville Centre	1977	46
Diocese of Baton Rouge	1977	15
Diocese of Houma-Thibodaux	1977	5
Eparchy of St. Maron, Brooklyn (Maronite)	1977	26
Diocese of Sioux City	1978	7
Diocese of Orange	1978	16
Diocese of Allentown	1978	24
Archdiocese of Oklahoma City	1978	22
Diocese of Orlando	1978	7
Diocese of Stockton	1978	13
Diocese of Fargo	1978	14
Diocese of Springfield in Massachusetts	1978	10
Diocese of Sacramento	1978	29
Diocese of Rochester	1978	17
Diocese of Norwich	1979	11
Diocese of Little Rock	1979	27
Archdiocese of Miami	1979	18
Diocese of San Bernardino	1979	0
Diocese of Bismarck	1980	8
Diocese of Austin	1980	34
Diocese of Dodge City	1980	8
Diocese of Marquette	1981	3
Diocese of Alexandria	1982	0
Diocese of Covington	1982	0
Archdiocese of Philadelphia	1983	48
Diocese of Fort Worth	1984	0
Diocese of Metuchen	1985	24
Diocese of Crookston	1985	6
Diocese of Altoona-Johnstown	1988	9

Diaconate Formation Programs by Date Founded and Enrollment, cont.

Diocese or Eparchy	Founded	Enrollment
Diocese of Scranton	1988	17
Diocese of Cheyenne	1989	8
Diocese of Santa Rosa	1990	20
Diocese of Lubbock	1992	N/A
Diocese of Lexington	1992	0
Diocese of Yakima	1993	0
Archdiocese of Portland in Oregon	1993	4
Eparchy of Our Lady of Lebanon (Maronite)	1994	2
Diocese of Salt Lake City	1994	5
Diocese of Portland in Maine	1994	0
Diocese of Columbus	1994	11
Diocese of St. Petersburg	1994	0
Diocese of Belleville	1994	0
Diocese of Erie	1994	22
Diocese of Tyler	1994	19
Archdiocese of San Francisco	1995	N/A
Diocese of Spokane	1995	0
Archdiocese of Santa Fe	1995	85
Diocese of Nashville	1995	0
Diocese of Pittsburgh	1995	2
Diocese of Helena	1996	7
Diocese of Las Cruces	1996	12
Diocese of Lake Charles	1996	24
Diocese of Baker	1996	14
Diocese of Boise	1996	17
Diocese of Pueblo	1996	11
Diocese of Memphis	1996	33
Diocese of Pensacola-Tallahassee	1996	18
Diocese of La Crosse	1997	10
Diocese of Birmingham	1997	19
Diocese of Manchester	1997	27
Diocese of Ogdensburg	1997	0
Diocese of Victoria	1997	8
Diocese of Colorado Springs	1998	9
Diocese of Honolulu	1998	20
Diocese of Oakland	1998	26
Diocese of Fresno	1999	25
Diocese of Santa Rosa	1999	N/A
Eparchy of Passaic (Byzantine)	1999	18

Table A.9. Lay Ecclesial Ministry Formation Programs by Date Founded, with 1999-2000 Enrollment

Lay Ministry Program	Institution Founded	Enrollment
St. Mary's Seminary and University School of Theology , Baltimore, MD	1791	6
Saint-Mary-of-the-Woods College BA in Theology, Saint Mary of the Woods, IN	1840	50
Graduate Degree Programs, Buffalo, NY	1857	77
Graduate Degree Programs, Collegeville, MN	1870	119
Lay Ministry Formation Program, Grand Rapids, MI	1886	30
Religious Studies Department, Spokane, WA	1887	50
Mayo Foundation CPE Program, Rochester, MN	1889	11
Institute for Ministry, Detroit, MI	1919	219
Religious Pastoral Ministry Program, Cincinnati, OH	1920	36
Graduate Program in Ministry, Cambridge, MA	1922	212
Aquinas Institute of Theology Graduate Degree Program, Saint Louis, MO	1925	211
Graduate Program in Religious Studies, Los Angeles, CA	1925	35
School of Religious Studies, Washington, DC	1930	N/A
Jesuit School of Theology - Masters Programs in Theology, Berkeley, CA	1934	56
Jesuit School of Theology - Graduate Degree Program, Berkeley, CA	1934	14
D.C. Commission on Mental Health CPE Program, Washington, DC	1944	8
Graduate Program in Theology, Pastoral, and Liturgy Studies, Philadelphia, PA	1950	N/A
Spalding University - Religious Studies Program, Russell Institute, Louisville, KY	1952	14
Pastoral Theology Program, San Antonio, TX	1960	71
School of Applied Theology, Oakland, CA	1960	51
MA in Theology Program, San Francisco, CA	1961	60
Graduate Theology and Pastoral Ministry Program, Colchester, VT	1961	60
Institute for Religious Education and Pastoral Studies (REAPS), Fairfield, CT	1963	191
Graduate School of Religion and Religious Education, Bronx, NY	1964	154
Loyola University of Chicago Institute of Pastoral Studies, Chicago, IL	1964	232
Pastoral Institute, Douglaston, NY	1967	N/A
Pastoral Institute, San Antonio, TX	1968	54
Catholic Theological Union, Chicago, IL	1968	253

Lay Ecclesial Ministry Formation Programs by Date Founded and 1999-2000 Enrollment, cont.

Lay Ministry Program	Founded	Enrollment
Catholic Theological Union Master of Arts in Pastoral Studies, Chicago, IL	1968	87
Graduate Degree Programs, Washington, DC	1968	269
Cherokee Mental Health Institute CPE Program, Cherokee, IA	1968	6
St. Mary's Seminary and University Ecumenical Institute of Theology, Baltimore, MD	1968	214
Loyola Institute for Ministry-(LIMEX) On-Campus Program, New Orleans, LA	1968	N/A
Master of Divinity Program, Notre Dame, IN	1968	37
Graduate Degree Programs, Berkeley, CA	1968	93
Department of Religious Studies, Dayton, OH	1969	112
Notre Dame Graduate School, Alexandria, VA	1969	174
Lay Graduate Degree Programs, Saint Meinrad, IN	1969	37
Graduate Program in Pastoral Studies, Erie, PA	1971	18
Institute for Religious Education and Pastoral Ministry, Chestnut Hill, MA	1971	164
Hispanic Pastoral Ministry Program, San Antonio, TX	1972	N/A
Kino Institute of Theology, Phoenix, AZ	1972	N/A
St. Francis Seminary - Lay Formation Program, Saint Francis, WI	1972	56
Lay Ministry Program, La Crosse, WI	1973	100
Instituto Hispano de Formacion Pastoral, New York, NY	1973	N/A
Lay Ministry Program, Orchard Lake, MI	1973	52
Institute for Spirituality and Worship, Berkeley, CA	1973	10
St. John's Regional Health Center CPE Program, Springfield, MO	1974	7
Holy Family Hospital and Medical Center CPE Program, Methuen, MA	1974	4
Lay Ministry Degree Program, South Orange, NJ	1974	105
Graduate Degree Programs, Huntington, NY	1974	100
MA in Theology Program, Saint Benedict, OR	1975	N/A
Lay Pastoral Ministry Program, Cincinnati, OH	1975	152
Interfaith Health Care Ministries CPE Program, Providence, RI	1975	10
Tri-Health Bethesda and Good Samaritan Hospital CPE Program, Cincinnati, OH	1975	8
Religion Studies Department, University Heights, OH	1975	21
Franciscan Skemp CPE Program, LaCrosse, WI	1975	7
Hispanic Lay Ministry Formation Program, Saginaw, MI	1976	N/A

Lay Ministry Program	Founded	Enrollment
Notre Dame College, South Euclid, OH	1976	92
School of Ministry, Miami Shores, FL	1977	106
Institute of Religious Studies, Yonkers, NY	1977	149
Ministry Formation Program, Toledo, OH	1977	146
Institute for Christian Ministries, San Diego, CA	1977	37
Loyola Institute for Ministry Extension (LIMEX) Program, Savannah, GA	1978	60
Trinity College Campus-Education for Parish Service Day Program, Washington, DC	1978	76
Loyola Institute for Ministry Extension (LIMEX) Program, Portland, ME	1978	N/A
Loyola Institute for Ministry Extension (LIMEX) Program, Lansing, MI	1978	N/A
Loyola Institute for Ministry Extension (LIMEX) Program, Springfield, MO	1978	N/A
Loyola Institute for Ministry Extension (LIMEX) Program, Salt Lake City, UT	1978	N/A
Loyola Institute for Ministry Extension (LIMEX) Program, Saint Louis, MO	1978	N/A
Loyola Institute for Ministry Extension (LIMEX) Program, Evansville, IN	1978	16
Pastoral Ministry Center, Loretto, PA	1978	N/A
Loyola Institute for Ministry Extension (LIMEX) Program, Kansas City, MO	1978	N/A
Loyola Institute for Ministry Extension (LIMEX) Program, Marquette, MI	1978	0
Loyola Institute for Ministry Extension (LIMEX) Program, Sacramento, CA	1978	48
Loyola Institute for Ministry Extension (LIMEX) Program, Las Cruces, NM	1978	8
Loyola Institute for Ministry Extension (LIMEX) Program, Youngstown, OH	1978	21
Loyola Institute for Ministry Extension (LIMEX) Program, Alexandria, LA	1978	14
Loyola Institute for Ministry Extension (LIMEX) Program, Jefferson City, MO	1978	8
Lay Ministry Formation Program, Saginaw, MI	1978	97
Loyola Institute for Ministry Extension (LIMEX) Program, Jacksonville, FL	1978	5
Loyola Institute for Ministry Extension (LIMEX) Program, Saginaw, MI	1978	22
Loyola Institute for Ministry Extension (LIMEX) Program, Pensacola, FL	1978	9
St. Paul Seminary School of Divinity, Saint Paul, MN	1978	54

Lay Ecclesial Ministry Formation Programs by Date Founded and 1999-2000 Enrollment, cont.

Lay Ministry Program	Founded	Enrollment
Loyola Institute for Ministry Extension (LIMEX) Program, Orlando, FL	1978	30
Pastoral Ministry Leadership Formation, Orlando, FL	1978	90
Loyola Institute for Ministry Extension (LIMEX) Program, Nashville, TN	1978	N/A
Loyola Institute for Ministry Extension (LIMEX) Program, Greenville, TN	1978	N/A
Loyola Institute for Ministry Extension (LIMEX) Program, Charlotte, NC	1978	N/A
Loyola Institute for Ministry Extension (LIMEX) Program, San Angelo, TX	1978	10
Loyola Institute for Ministry Extension (LIMEX) Program, Madison, WI	1978	15
Institute for Pastoral Ministry, Orange, CA	1978	300
Loyola Institute for Ministry Extension (LIMEX) Program, Charleston, SC	1978	12
Center for Catholic Lay Leadership Formation, Bronx, NY	1978	124
Loyola Institute for Ministry Extension (LIMEX) Program, Stockton, CA	1978	9
Loyola Institute for Ministry Extension (LIMEX) Program, Shreveport, LA	1978	13
Loyola Institute for Ministry Extension (LIMEX) Program, Monterey, CA	1978	N/A
Loyola Institute for Ministry Extension (LIMEX) Program, Palmer, AK	1978	N/A
Loyola Institute for Ministry Extension (LIMEX) Program, Indianapolis, IN	1978	25
Brescia University Off-Campus Ministry Formation Program, Evansville, IN	1978	59
Loyola Institute for Ministry Extension (LIMEX) Program, Little Rock, AR	1978	N/A
Loyola Institute for Ministry (LIM) Program, New Orleans, LA	1978	847
Loyola Institute for Ministry Extension (LIMEX) Program, Wilmington, DE	1978	36
Loyola Institute for Ministry Extension (LIMEX) Program, North Platte, NE	1978	17
Loyola Institute for Ministry Extension (LIMEX) Program, La Crosse, WI	1978	N/A
Loyola Institute for Ministry Extension (LIMEX) Program, Raleigh, NC	1978	19

Lay Ministry Program	Founded	Enrollment
Loyola Institute for Ministry Extension (LIMEX) Program, Lake Charles, LA	1978	N/A
Loyola Institute for Ministry Extension (LIMEX) Program, Hollidaysburg, PA	1978	11
Loyola Institute for Ministry Extension (LIMEX) Program, Lafayette, LA	1978	N/A
Loyola Institute for Ministry Extension (LIMEX) Program, Baton Rouge, LA	1978	N/A
Loyola Institute for Ministry Extension (LIMEX) Program, Omaha, NE	1978	10
Loyola Institute for Ministry Extension (LIMEX) Program, Toledo, OH	1978	38
Loyola Institute for Ministry Extension (LIMEX) Program, Grand Rapids, MI	1978	5
Loyola Institute for Ministry Extension (LIMEX) Program, Richmond, VA	1978	41
Loyola Institute for Ministry Extension (LIMEX) Program, Kansas City, KS	1978	0
Pastoral Ministry Office, Wickliffe, OH	1979	97
Lay Ministry Formation Program, Dubuque, IA	1979	N/A
Ministry Institute, Providence, RI	1979	20
Ministry Formation Program, Jefferson City, MO	1980	96
MA in Theology, Steubenville, OH	1980	125
BA in Ministry, La Crosse, WI	1980	N/A
Southeast Pastoral Institute (SEPI), Miami, FL	1980	N/A
Formation for Ministry, Syracuse, NY	1980	120
MA in Applied Theology, Chicopee, MA	1980	18
Pastoral Ministry/Catechist Certification Program, Biloxi, MS	1980	350
Ministry Certification Program, Milwaukee, WI	1980	50
Pastoral Ministry Program, Saint Paul, MN	1980	22
MA in Pastoral Ministry, Detroit, MI	1981	51
Christus Santa Rosa Health Care CPE Program, San Antonio, TX	1981	4
Graduate Program in Community Leadership, Denver, CO	1981	30
Lamp Ministries, Bronx, NY	1981	19
Ministry Formation Program, Uncasville, CT	1981	33
Spring Hill College - Master in Theological Studies Program, Mobile, AL	1981	135
MA in Pastoral Ministries, Miami, FL	1981	31
St. Joseph Medical Center CPE Program, Tacoma, WA	1981	25
Toolen Institute for Parish Services, Mobile, AL	1981	27
St. Bernard's Institute, Rochester, NY	1981	103

Lay Ecclesial Ministry Formation Programs by Date Founded and 1999-2000 Enrollment, cont.

Lay Ministry Program	Founded	Enrollment
Brooklyn Catholic Charities CPE Program, Brooklyn, NY	1982	14
Loyola Marymount University - MA in Pastoral Studies, Los Angeles, CA	1982	N/A
St. Elizabeth's Medical Center CPE Program, Brighton, MA	1982	37
Lay Ministry Leadership Program, Peoria, IL	1982	29
Our Lady of the New Advent Theological Institute Catholic Biblical School, Denver, CO	1982	527
Religious Studies Institute, Baton Rouge, LA	1982	82
Education for Parish Service (EPS)Virginia Program, Falls Church, VA	1982	50
Program of Formation for Lay Ministers, Helena, MT	1982	33
Graduate Program in Pastoral Ministry and Religious Education, Duquesne University, Pittsburgh, PA	1982	46
Institute for Ministry Formation (English), Sacramento, CA	1982	118
Lay Ministries Leadership School, Marquette, MI	1982	18
Oblate School of Theology - Lay Ministry Institute, San Antonio, TX	1982	47
Instituto de Liderazgo Pastoral, Oak Park, IL	1982	75
Formation Program, San Angelo, TX	1982	99
Spring Hill College Extension Site - Master in Theological Studies, Jackson, MS	1982	21
Church Ministry Program, Wynnewood, PA	1982	134
Lay Ministry Program, Newington, CT	1983	28
Education for Parish Service (EPS) Connecticut Program, Stamford, CT	1983	95
Sisters of Mercy Institute for Religious Education and Lay Ministry, Erie, PA	1983	N/A
Pastoral Ministry Program, Oklahoma City, OK	1983	166
Graduate in Pastoral Ministries, Santa Clara, CA	1983	92
Formation for Christian Service, Albuquerque, NM	1984	453
Trinity College - Education for Parish Service (EPS) Evening Program, Washington, DC	1984	154
Ministry Programs, Morristown, NJ	1984	149
Hispanic Pastoral Ministry, Los Angeles, CA	1984	20
Pastoral Formation Institute, Dalton, PA	1984	2,000
Formation for Ministry Program, Albany, NY	1984	97
Saint-Mary-of-the-Woods College -Graduate Program in Pastoral Theology, Saint Mary of the Woods, IN	1984	60

Lay Ministry Program	Founded	Enrollment
Christian Foundations for Ministry, Newark, NJ	1984	435
Greco Institute, Shreveport, LA	1985	434
New Wine: Diocesan Formation for Ministry, Kansas City, MO	1985	117
Ministry Formation Program, Kalamazoo, MI	1985	55
Brescia University, Owensboro, KY	1985	38
Escuela de Liderazgo y Ministerios Hispanos, Rockford, IL	1985	607
Loyola Institute for Ministry Extension (LIMEX) Program, Marietta, GA	1985	N/A
Oblate School of Theology - Instituto de Formacion Pastoral, San Antonio, TX	1985	113
MA in Theology, Wickliffe, OH	1985	39
Seattle University School of Theology and Ministry, Seattle, WA	1985	282
Education for Parish Service (EPS) Vincent Pallotti Institute, Rome, Italy	1985	89
Lay Ministry Formation, Columbus, OH	1986	146
Parish Ministry Formation Program, Spokane, WA	1986	80
Pastoral Leadership Program, Romeoville, IL	1986	12
St. Mary's Medical Center CPE Program, Duluth, MN	1986	21
Lay Ministry Formation/Servant Leadership Program, Kaneohe, Oahu, HI	1986	700
Institute in Pastoral Ministries, Winona, MN	1986	55
Commissioned Leadership Formation Program, Green Bay, WI	1986	114
Pastoral Ministry Formation Office/Ministry Development Program, Covington, KY	1986	15
The Tempus Program, Great Falls, MT	1986	20
University of Dallas - Institute for Religious and Pastoral Studies, Irving, TX	1987	198
Graduate Certificate in Spiritual Direction and/or Directed Retreat, Omaha, NE	1987	N/A
MA in Theology, Hales Corners, WI	1987	23
Ministry Formation Program, Louisville, KY	1987	71
Masters of Theological Studies Program, De Pere, WI	1987	N/A
Certificate Youth Ministry Studies, Grand Rapids, MI	1987	N/A
Masters Program in Christian Spirituality, Omaha, NE	1987	N/A
Pastoral Institute, Victoria, TX	1987	191
Lay Ministry Formation Program, Rockford, IL	1987	157
Capacitacion Pastoral Instituto Hispano, Romeoville, IL	1987	70
Undergraduate Certificate Programs in Ministry, Spirituality, Theology and Liturgy, Omaha, NE	1987	N/A
Formacion Para El Ministerio Cristiano, Houston, TX	1988	250

Lay Ecclesial Ministry Formation Programs by Date Founded and 1999-2000 Enrollment, cont.

Lay Ministry Program	Founded	Enrollment
Loyola Institute for Ministry Extension (LIMEX) Program, Houma, LA	1988	17
Institute for Contemporary Spirituality, Scranton, PA	1988	14
Hispanic Institute in Theological and Pastoral Studies, Berkeley, CA	1988	48
Religious Studies Program, Salina, KS	1988	243
Notre Dame College, The Ministry Institute, Manchester, NH	1988	N/A
Pastoral Formation Institute, Rockville Centre, NY	1988	360
St. Francis Seminary Lay Ministry Certificate Division, Saint Francis, WI	1988	32
Church Ministries Program, Sioux City, IA	1988	23
Pastoral Formation Institute, Rockville Centre, NY	1989	350
Loyola Institute for Ministry Extension (LIMEX) Program, Syracuse, NY	1989	33
Lay Ministry Formation Program, Casper, WY	1989	28
Native American Lay Ministry Formation, Chinle, AZ	1989	76
Department of Theology and Master of Pastoral Studies, Davenport, IA	1989	N/A
Kateri Northwest Ministry Institute, Spokane, WA	1989	55
Lay Ministry Training Program, Charlotte, NC	1989	132
The Catholic Distance University, Hamilton, VA	1989	N/A
Tepeyac Institute, El Paso, TX	1989	N/A
Spalding University - Ministry Studies Program, Russell Institute, Louisville, KY	1989	75
Pastoral Ministry Formation Program, Atlanta, GA	1989	43
Leaven Program, Pensacola, FL	1989	66
St. Bernard's Institute - M.A./M.Div. Programs - Extension site, Albany, NY	1989	40
Foundations for Ministry Program, Baton Rouge, LA	1989	120
Ministry Formation Program, Lexington, KY	1990	27
Institute for Religious Studies, Atchison, KS	1990	278
Catholic Health Initiatives Organization CPE Program, Langhorne, PA	1990	25
DAYSTAR Program, Bridgeport, CT	1990	37
MA in Ministry Program, Pepper Pike, OH	1990	58
Formation for Ministry, Odensburg, NY	1990	94
"Comunidades Evangelizadoras" Lay Ministry Formation Program, Portland, OR	1990	42
Masters of Theological Studies, Fort Wayne, IN	1990	26
Spirituality Programs, Philadelphia, PA	1990	61

Lay Ministry Program	Founded	Enrollment
Lay Ministry Training Program, Erie, PA	1990	N/A
African American Catholic Ministries Program, Baltimore, MD	1990	N/A
Spring Hill College Extension, Birmingham, AL	1991	20
Ministry Formation Program, Saint Cloud, MN	1991	50
Lay Ministry Formation Program, Howes, SD	1991	70
Institute for Ministry, Gaylord, MI	1991	87
Pastoral Theology Programs, Houston, TX	1991	314
Lay Ministry Formation Program, Raleigh, NC	1991	97
Office for Lay Ministry, Springfield, IL	1991	39
Education for Ministry, Fort Wayne, IN	1991	90
Religious Studies Program, Wichita, KS	1991	N/A
St. Bernard's Institute - Certificate Programs, Rochester, NY	1992	84
Ministry Formation Program, Jacksonville, FL	1992	77
Lay Ministry Formation Process, Hollidaysburg, PA	1992	N/A
School of Ministry, Stockton, CA	1992	234
Lay Ministry Formation Programs, Granby, MA	1992	N/A
Loyola Institute for Ministry Extension (LIMEX) Program, Fort Belvoir, VA	1992	N/A
Loyola Marymount University - Hispanic Ministry Programs, Los Angeles, CA	1992	27
Aquinas Institute of Theology - MA in Pastoral Ministry Program, Oklahoma City, OK	1993	N/A
Ministry Programs, Austin, TX	1993	0
Loyola Institute for Ministry Extension (LIMEX) Program, Boise, ID	1993	13
San Diego Diocesan Institute, San Diego, CA	1993	650
Lay Ministry Outreach Formation Program, Superior, WI	1993	44
Catholic Institute for Evangelization, Philadelphia, PA	1993	280
Education and Ministry Collaborative, Worcester, MA	1993	723
Loyola University Medical Center CPE Program, Maywood, IL	1993	11
Diocesan Pastoral Leadership Program, Crookston, MN	1993	57
Ministry Formation Program, La Grange, IL	1993	18
Graduate Pastoral Education Program, Dubuque, IA	1994	N/A
The School of Pastoral Leadership, San Francisco, CA	1994	560
Lay Ministry Formation Program, Saint Louis, MO	1994	59
Leadership Ministry Formation Program, Pueblo, CO	1994	33
Education for Parish Service (EPS) Florida Program, Naples, FL	1994	99
Programa Hispano de Formacion Ministerial, Yakima, WA	1994	110

Lay Ecclesial Ministry Formation Programs by Date Founded and 1999-2000 Enrollment, cont.

Lay Ministry Program	Founded	Enrollment
University of Dallas - Masters in Ministry Program, Portland, OR	1994	N/A
Ministry Formation Program, Merrillville, IN	1994	60
Institute of Pastoral Ministry, Canyon, TX	1994	25
Ministry Training Program, Stowe, VT	1994	18
Institute for Ministries, Pittsburgh, PA	1994	30
Hispanic Formation Institute-Spanish, Sacramento, CA	1995	110
Instituto Hispano de Liturgia, Chicago, IL	1995	25
Ministry Formation Program, Portland, OR	1995	N/A
Ministry Formation Program, Lansing, MI	1995	70
Rice School for Pastoral Ministry, Arcadia, FL	1995	126
Partners in Ministry, East Brunswick, NJ	1995	22
Lay Ministry Program, Anchorage, AK	1995	N/A
Lay Ministry Formation Program, Little Rock, AR	1995	70
St. Anne's Hospital CPE Program, Fall River, MA	1995	14
New Wine Ministry Formation Program, Romeoville, IL	1995	15
Institute of Ministry and Leadership, Reno, NV	1995	35
Loyola Institute for Ministry Extension (LIMEX) Program, Columbus, OH	1995	N/A
People of God Ministry Program, Steubenville, OH	1995	122
Lay Ministry Training Program, Youngstown, OH	1995	154
Light of Christ Institute for Lay Ministry Formation, Fort Worth, TX	1996	N/A
Loyola University of New Orleans Certificate in Advanced Studies (CAS), New Orleans, LA	1996	9
Certificate of Advanced Studies (CAS), Saginaw, MI	1996	26
Certificate of Advanced Studies (CAS), Grand Rapids, MI	1996	0
Christ the Servant Lay Institute, Dallas, TX	1996	300
Diocesan Lay Ministry Program, Schriever, LA	1996	56
New Wine Program, Fresno, CA	1996	46
Certificate of Advanced Studies (CAS), Lake Charles, LA	1996	10
Certificate of Advanced Studies (CAS),Savannah, GA	1996	15
Certificate of Advanced Studies (CAS), Raleigh, NC	1996	18
Certificate of Advanced Studies (CAS), Richmond, VA	1996	3
Certificate of Advanced Studies (CAS), Salt Lake City, UT	1996	0
Education for Parish Service (EPS), New York, NY	1996	208

Lay Ministry Program	Founded	Enrollment
Certificate of Advanced Studies (CAS), Knoxville, TN	1996	9
Ministry Formation Program, Davenport, IA	1997	103
The Caldwell Pastoral Ministry Institute, Caldwell, NJ	1997	35
Institute for Leadership in Ministry, Santa Clara, CA	1997	220
Lay Ministry Foundation Program, Augusta, ME	1997	31
Institute for Christian Life and Ministry, St. Paul, MN	1997	160
Institute of Religious Studies, Sioux Falls, SD	1998	1,300
Loyola University of New Orleans Loyola Pastoral Life Center, New Orleans, LA	1998	N/A
Church Leadership Institute, Baltimore, MD	1998	252
Skills For Ministry Leadership Program, Lubbock, TX	1998	105
Pastoral Office for Formation, Lafayette, IN	1998	35
Lay Ministry Program, Harrisburg, PA	1998	55
Lay Ministy Formation, Saint Petersburg, FL	1998	147
Lay Leadership Formation for the Diocese of Grand Rapids, Grand Rapids, MI	1999	N/A
Our Lady of the New Advent Theological Institute - Catechetical School, Denver, CO	1999	1,800
Lay Ministry Certification Program, Great Falls, MT	1999	11
Office of Pastoral Services, Madison, WI	2000	0

Notes

1. THE CATHOLIC POPULATION

1. Here and throughout this book Catholic population figures are based on what is reported by dioceses and parishes, rather than self-identified Catholics as in national surveys. This allows for a more complete analysis, as well as more conservative estimates. We exclude Puerto Rico and other U.S. territories such as Micronesia from population figures. Only the bishops within the fifty states and the District of Columbia are members of the United States Conference of Catholic Bishops (USCCB), with the exception of the bishop of the U.S. Virgin Islands.

Table 1.1 figures are compiled from *The Official Catholic Directory 1999*, the *1999 Yearbook of American and Canadian Churches*, and the U.S. Census. It is important to note that the figures in *The Official Catholic Directory* are based on parish membership as reported by individual parishes. According to these estimates, Catholics constitute 22 percent of the population. However, estimates of the Catholic population based on self-identification find that Catholics comprise a somewhat larger percentage of the U.S. population. Barry A. Kosmin and Seymour P. Lachman, authors of *One Nation Under God* (New York: Crown Trade Paperbacks, 1993), report that 26 percent of the respondents in their massive National Survey of Religious Identification identify themselves as Catholic. Gallup Polls from April and September 1999 report Catholics to be even higher, at 27 and 28 percent, respectively. The large national surveys used by social scientists, such as the General Social Surveys of the National Opinion Research Center at the University of Chicago and the American National Election Studies of the Center for Political Studies at the University of Michigan, typically find that Catholics comprise around 25 percent.

2. Martin B. Bradley et al., 1992, *Churches and Church Membership in the United States 1990: An Enumeration by Region, State and County Based on Data Reported for 133 Church Groupings*, Atlanta, Georgia, Glenmary Research Center, Table 1.

3. Table 1.2 figures are compiled from the *Annuarium Statisticum Ecclesiae*, 1997.

4. Where possible, the data used in the table that follows is directly provided by the religious body and subject to double-checking by CARA. Where that was not possible, information provided by the religious body to the *1999 Yearbook of American and Canadian Religious Bodies* was used.

5. Charles R. Morris, 1997, *American Catholic: The Saints and Sinners Who Built America's Most Powerful Church*, USA: Random House/Times Books.

6. Cyprian Davis, OSB, 1990, *The History of Black Catholics in the United States*, New York: Crossroad; for further reading, see Diana L. Hayes and Cyprian Davis, eds., 1998, *Taking Down Our Harps: Black Catholics in the United States*, Maryknoll, N.Y.: Orbis Books.

7. Table 1.4 is compiled from Martin B. Bradley et al., 1992, *Churches and Church Membership in the United States.*

8. See William H. Newman and and Peter L Halvorson, 2000, *Atlas of American Religion: The Denominational Era, 1776-1990*, Walnut Creek: Altamira Press, 69-72 and 76-79.

9. The figures given on immigrant country of origin in Table 1.6 should be interpreted with caution. First, the data come from reports of immigration officials rather than the immigrants themselves. Second, since they report the country of origin according to the territorial division of Europe at the time, national groupings do not present an accurate picture. For example, large numbers of Poles entered the U.S. from Germany, Austria-Hungary, and Russia. Figures are from Louis J. Putz, CSC, ed., 1956, *The Catholic Church, U.S.A.*, Fides Publishers, 157. Some historical information is also available from the U.S. Department of Justice web site, at www.ins.usdoj.gov/graphics/aboutins/statistics/index.htm.

10. Private correspondence with David Leege.

11. The number of immigrants has risen from 2.1 per thousand people in 1970 to 3.5 per thousand in 1993 according to the U.S. Census Bureau, *Statistical Abstract of the United States: 1998*, No. 8.

12. Ana María Díaz-Stevens and Anthony M. Stevens-Arroyo, 1998, *Recognizing the Latino Religious Insurgence in U.S. Religion: The Emmaus Paradigm*, U.S.A.: Westview Press.

13. Contrary to stereotypical portrayals, the Italian population (immigrant and settled) in the United States at the turn of the century was no more a homogeneous group of Catholics than the Hispanic/Latino population is today. Of European immigrants at the turn of the twentieth century, Italians were the least likely to remain Catholic, due to several factors. A large proportion of Italian immigrants were young, single men who had adopted the anticlerical politics of the day, or at the very least were not particularly diligent Catholic practitioners. Protestant religions were seen as a method of "Americanization," which a significant number of working-class Italians were ready to adopt as a means of bettering their condition. Italian immigrants and Italian Americans were also far more likely to "marry out" of their ethnic group and their nominal religious affiliation; many of these single men married Protestant women, thus altering the religious affiliation of their children. See Charles R. Morris, 1997, *American Catholic.*

14. Table 1.8 is from data reported in *The Official Catholic Directory* (OCD) for those years. Note that the OCD publishes figures for the calendar year prior to its publication year. Thus, the 1999 OCD actually presents data as of January 1, 1998.

15. U.S. Census Bureau, *Statistical Abstract of the United States 1998*, No. 61, "Marital Status of the Population by Sex, Race and Hispanic Origin, 1980 to 1997."

16. Robert Emmett Curran, SJ, 1993, *The Bicentennial History of Georgetown University,* vol. 1, *From Academy to University*, Washington, D.C.: Georgetown University Press. The quote is from Bishop Carroll's 1787 appeal to the "Reverend Gentlemen of the Southern District, Maryland," and from a broadside of that same year, "Proposals for Establishing an Academy at George-Town, Patowmack River, Maryland" (see pages 1, 15, 17 and 26).

17. These data are taken from the CARA Catholic Poll 2000.

18. A. M. Díaz-Stevens and A. Stevens-Arroyo, 1998, *Recognizing the Latino Religious Resurgence*, 14ff.

19. See W. M. Newman and P. L. Halvorson, *Atlas of American Religion*.

20. James D. Davidson, et al., 1997, *The Search for Common Ground: What Unites and Divides Catholic Americans*, Our Sunday Visitor, Inc., 195.

2. CATHOLIC BEHAVIOR AND VALUES

1. See, for example, William V. D'Antonio et al., 1989, *American Catholic Laity in a Changing Church*, Sheed and Ward; and William V. D'Antonio, et al., 1996, Laity, American and Catholic: Transforming the Church, Sheed and Ward.

2. James D. Davidson, et al., 1997, *The Search for Common Ground: What Unites and Divides Catholic Americans*, Our Sunday Visitor, Inc.

3. Gerhard Lenski, 1963 (1961), *The Religious Factor: A Sociologist's Inquiry*, Garden City, NY: Anchor Books/Doubleday.

4. James D. Davidson, et al., 1997, *The Search for Common Ground*, 178-180. Traditionally, all Catholics living within the geographical boundaries of a parish were considered members by default; however, current practices require that Catholics register formally with their parish, as they would with any voluntary association. Some 31 percent of the self-defined Catholic respondents to the survey conducted by the book's authors stated that they were not "registered as a member of a Catholic parish near where you live." Fourteen percent of the total sample reported no relation with any parish whatsoever, and 17 percent of the total sample (47 percent of those claiming no formal affiliation with a parish) reported having an "informal relation" with the parish.

5. Metropolitan and non-metropolitan rates are computed from the *National Parish Inventory*, CARA, 1999.

6. Dean R. Hoge, 1999, "What is most central to being a Catholic?" *National Catholic Reporter*, vol. 36, no. 2 (October 29, 1999). This article, and several others in the same issue of the *National Catholic Reporter*, presents the preliminary findings of the third wave of the study of U.S. Catholics by D'Antonio, Davidson, Hoge, and Wallace. For the most recent study, Kathleen Meyer replaced Ruth A. Wallace as a member of the research team.

7. George Gallup, Jr., *The People's Religion: American Faith in the 90s*, New York: Macmillan Publishing Co. and George Gallup Jr. and Jim Castelli, 1987, *The American Catholic People: Their Beliefs, Practices, and Values*, Garden City, NY: Doubleday and Co., Inc.

8. Andrew Greeley, 1981, *The Religious Imagination*, New York: William H. Sadlier, and 1995, *Religion as Poetry*, New Brunswick: NJ: Transaction Publications; the information for Table 2.8 is taken from Greeley's work. Also see John E. Tropman, 1995, *The Catholic Ethic in American Society: An Exploration of Values*, San Francisco: Jossey-Bass Publishers. The contemporary data for this section comes from Mary E. Bendyna, R.S.M., 1999, *The Catholic Ethic in American Politics: Evidence from Survey Research*, Ph.D. dissertation, Georgetown University.

3. DIOCESES AND PARISHES

1. Figures for Catholic population and clergy before 1800 are from Gerald Shaughnessy, 1969 (1925), *Has the Immigrant Kept the Faith? A Study of Immigration and Catholic Growth in the United States, 1790 to 1920*, New York: Arno Press. Table 3.1 numbers after 1850 are compiled from *The Official Catholic Directory* and the U.S. Census for those years. The total number of dioceses in 1998 does not include the Archdiocese for the Military Services or the Diocese of St. Thomas in the Virgin Islands, consistent with the rest of this book, and their numbers are not included in the other figures for that row.

2. In October 2000, the National Conference of Catholic Bishops (NCCB), as it has been known since its establishment in 1966,will adopt the new title of USCCB, which CARA has used for the preparation of this book. The NCCB, a canonical organization of bishops, and the United States Catholic Conference (USCC), a civil corporation of laity and clergy, were organized from the National Catholic Welfare Conference, founded in 1919. For more information on the origins of the NCCB, see Chapter 5.

3. For an introduction to the Eastern Churches, see Joan L. Roccasalvo, 1992, *The Eastern Catholic Churches: An Introduction to Their Worship and Spirituality*, Collegeville, MN: Liturgical Press; for more detailed information, see John D. Faris, 1992, *The Eastern Catholic Churches: Constitution and Governance According to the Code of Canons of the Eastern Churches*, New York: Saint Maron Publications.

4. Table 3.4 figures are from *The Official Catholic Directory*, 1999, and reflect totals as of 1998.

5. Table 3.5 region totals do not include Catholics of the Archeparchies and Eparchies of the Eastern Churches (446,445 Catholics). While they are included organizationally within the various USCCB regions, their territorial boundaries are much broader than some of these regions, occasionally including the entire territory of the United States.

6. The Code of Canon Law is actually a compilation of the totality of Church law, from its earliest days to the present. Compiling a universal collection of Catholic Church law had been attempted since the Middle Ages, when Gratian (a Camadolese monk teaching at the university of Bologna) produced his *Concordia Discordantium Canonum* in about 1141, giving the first systematic, scientific approach to the laws of the Church. The first *Codex Iuris Canonici* was promulgated by Gregory XIII in 1582, but subsequent decrees and laws were not integrated into it. The First Vatican Council (1869-1879) established as one of its goals a much-needed reform of canon law. Political struggles in Italy interrupted this work, which Pope Pius X ordered resumed on March 19, 1904. The first complete *Corpus Iuris Canonici* was promulgated on the Pentecost Sunday of 27 May 1917, and went into effect one year later. One of the decrees of the Second Vatican Council (1962-1965) was to revise the Code, in order to bring it into harmony with the conciliar reforms. This work was not completed until 1983; the Code was promulgated on 25 January (the feast of the conversion of St. Paul,

considered to be the Church's first jurist) and went into effect on 27 November, the First Sunday of Advent. The official version of the Code is the Latin version; however, for the English translation of the Code, plus useful histories and explanations, see James A. Coriden, Thomas J. Green, and Donald E. Heintshel, 1985, *The Code of Canon Law: A Text and Commentary* New York: Paulist Press/The Canon Law Society of America. For quick reference one can also consult the Code online at http://www.prairienet.org/nrpcatholic/cicmenu.html. In this volume, as is standard, all citations of the Code will be made with parenthetical references to its numbered sections, noted with "c." (e.g., "c. 515.1").

7. Tables 3.8 and 3.9 totals do not include Catholics of the Archeparchies and Eparchies of the Eastern Churches because it is not possible to calculate total population (and thus percent Catholic) for their very broad geographical boundaries.

8. In fact, nine of the ten dioceses with the lowest Catholic population densities are in the states of the old Confederacy. Most Catholic immigrants in the nineteenth and early twentieth centuries originally settled in urban areas of the Northeast and Upper Midwest, attracted there by jobs and an already established Catholic presence. Except for the Catholic settlements in New Orleans and along the Louisiana Gulf coast, few Catholics chose to settle in the less inviting conditions of the Southeast at that time.

9. On the other hand, Catholic Mass attendance has declined by about half during this period.

10. Using the latest available census data (*U.S. Statistical Abstracts 1998*) for the population of the United States, this quantity of registered parishioners works out to about 22.1 percent of the U.S. population (59,156,237 out of 267,636,061). Considering the estimates of Gallup Polls and B. Kosmin and S. Lachman, the population of people who self-identify as Catholic may be higher: 27 or 28 percent (roughly 72 or 75 million), or 69.5 million, respectively.

11. In 1996 (the latest date available), 79.8 percent of people in the United States lived in metropolitan areas as defined by the U.S. Bureau of the Census. See *Statistical Abstract of the U.S. 1998*, No. 40.

12. The single criterion used was the number of registered parishioners. No attempt is made here to distinguish parishes that are twinned or clustered with another parish to share parish staff. Mission parishes are counted as discrete parishes, as long as they were reported to be autonomous parishes by their diocese or eparchy.

13. The ratio of infant baptisms to funerals provides a helpful way to understand the general age structure of a parish. Although there are limitations to this approach, Church researchers have found it to be a helpful predictor of a parish's age distribution and population growth.

14. Table 3.18 reports numbers of parishes who responded to the National Parish Inventory question about ethnic or national identification and parishes so identified in *The Official Catholic Directory*.

15. Calculated from diocesan figures collected by CARA in 1999.

4. CATHOLIC EDUCATION

1. Technically, a distinction could be made for different types of religious institutes discussed in this chapter. The term "religious orders" has a specific historical meaning that at one point set them apart from religious congregations. At the time, all women's religious institutes were congregations in the sense that their members only took simple vows, as opposed to members of religious orders, restricted to men, who took solemn vows. However, the use of "religious orders" as a general term to describe many women's and men's religious institutes is so common that for the sake of ease in reading it will be used in the text. See Chapter 7, "Women and Men Religious."

2. This section owes much to Anthony S. Bryk, Valerie E. Lee and Peter B. Holland, 1993, *Catholic Schools and the Common Good*, Cambridge, MA: Harvard University Press, and Jay P. Dolan, SJ, 1992, *The American Catholic Experience: A History from Colonial Times to the Present*, Notre Dame, IN: University of Notre Dame Press, as well as Rev. J.A. Burns, CSC, 1912, *The Growth and Development of the Catholic School System in the United States*, New York: Benziger Brothers, and Matthew Burnson, ed., 1999, *Our Sunday Visitor's Catholic Almanac 2000*, Huntington, IN: Our Sunday Visitor.

3. This summary is computed from the total number of infant baptisms for each year, as reported in *The Official Catholic Directory* (*OCD*). It assumes that children reported baptized in one year were born in the previous calendar year. For example, children reported as infant baptisms in the 1999 *OCD* are assumed to have been born in calendar year 1998.

4. Figures for enrollments and schools are calculated from diocesan totals reported in the 1951 and 1999 *OCD*. Estimated K-8 children is computed by summing the numbers of baptisms in all dioceses for the appropriate years. For example, the estimated numbers of K-8 children in 1950 is the sum of all baptisms between 1936 and 1944.

5. Figures for enrollments and schools are calculated from diocesan totals reported in the 1951 and 1999 *OCD*. Estimated 9-12 children is computed by summing the numbers of baptisms in all dioceses for the appropriate years (1932-1935 for the 1950 group, and 1980-1983 for the 1998 group).

6. Table 4.4 uses *OCD* figures to represent total elementary and high school teachers. The figures from *OCD* also do not distinguish between diocesan and religious priest teachers. Most priest teachers are religious priests, but some diocesan high schools, in particular, employ diocesan priests as teachers.

7. Pius X, *Acerbo Nimis* (On Teaching Christian Doctrine), 15 April 1905 (at www.ewtn.com/library/ENCYC/P10CHDOC.HTM); also see listings in the *Catholic Almanac 2000*. The CCD also licenses use of the Lectionary for Mass and the New American Bible (translations made from the original languages in accordance with Pius XII's 1943 papal encyclical *Divino Afflante Spiritu* (On Promoting Biblical Studies). For more on the history of Catholic charitable agencies, see Chapter 5.

8. Information for the text and following charts are from recent CARA studies of diocesan programs of religious education; see Bryan T. Froehle and Mary E. Bendyna, RSM, 1999, *Diocesan Profile of Catechetical Ministry: An NCCL, NCEA and USCC Joint Project*, Washington, D.C.: Center for Applied Research in the Apostolate. Also see James D. Davidson et al., 1997, *The Search for Common Ground: What Unites and Divides Catholic Americans*, Huntington, Ind., Our Sunday Visitor, Inc., Chapter 6, "Religious Formation."

9. See the "U.S. News and World Report: 1999 College Rankings," 1999, available at www.usnews.com/usnews/edu/college/corank.htm.

10. This section owes much to J. P. Dolan, SJ, 1992, *The American Catholic Experience*, and to Chester Gillis, 1999, *Roman Catholicism in America*, New York: Columbia University Press, Chapter 9, "Challenges." Also see John Paul II, *Ex Corde Ecclesiae*, 15 Aug. 1990 (at www.cin.org/jp2/excorde.html and www.ewtn.com/library/PAPALDOC/JP2/UNIVE.HTM), and John P. Langan, S.J., ed., 1993, *Catholic Universities in Church and Society: A Dialogue on Ex Corde Ecclesiae*, Washington, D.C.: Georgetown University Press.

11. Private communication with Sandy Ivers, Member Services and Communications Director of the Catholic Campus Ministry Association, February 18, 2000. Also see the Catholic Newman Center at Temple University website, www.templenewmancenter.org/index.html.

5. SOCIAL SERVICE INSTITUTIONS AND AGENCIES

1. Background information for this section was taken from Jay P. Dolan, SJ, 1992, *The American Catholic Experience: A History from Colonial Times to the Present*, Notre Dame, Indiana: Notre Dame University Press; Chester Gillis, 1999, *Roman Catholicism in America*, New York: Columbia University Press; George C. Stewart, Jr., 1994, *Marvels of Charity: History of American Sisters and Nuns*, Huntington, Ind.: Our Sunday Visitor, Inc.; and the website of the Catholic Health Association of the United States, www.chausa.org.

2. These comparative figures on Catholic hospitals and health care agencies are summaries of diocesan figures reported in *The Official Catholic Directory*, 1951 and 1999.

3. From Richard A. McCormick, SJ, "The End of Catholic Hospitals?" in *America*, July 4, 1998. More than 2,000 Catholic-sponsored facilities and organizations are represented by the Catholic Health Association (www.chausa.org [14 Feb. 2000]).

4. The NCSSS was absorbed into Catholic University's School of Social Work after World War II.

5. Excellent resources for exploring the history and organizational structure of Catholic Charities include: Dorothy Brown and Elizabeth McKeown, 1997, *The Poor Belong to Us: Catholic Charities and American Welfare*, Cambridge, Mass. and London, England, Harvard University Press; Donald P. Gavin, 1962, *The National Conference of Catholic Charities, 1910-1960*, Milwaukee: Catholic Life Publications/Bruce Press; Mary J. Oates, 1995, *The Catholic Philanthropic*

Tradition in America, Bloomington and Indianapolis: Indiana University Press; Msgr. Edward J. Ryle, 1997, "Catholic Charities, Catholic Identity, and the Mission of the Church: Some Approaches for Catholic Charities," in *Who Do You Say We Are? Perspectives on Catholic Identity in Catholic Charities,* Alexandria, Va.: Catholic Charities USA, 1997; and the Catholic Charities USA website, www.catholiccharitiesusa.org.

6. Campaign for Human Development, 1995, *1994-95 Annual Report,* Washington, DC: United States Catholic Conference, Inc.; Catholic Campaign for Human Development (CCHD), 1998, *1997-98 Annual Report,* Washington, DC: United States Catholic Conference, Inc., 1998; CCHD, 1999, *Helping People Help Themselves: 1998-99 Annual Report,* Washington, DC: United States Catholic Conference, Inc.

7. Information for this section was drawn from Eileen Egan, 1988, *Catholic Relief Services: The Beginning Years: For the Life of the World,* New York, New York: Catholic Relief Services; Catholic Relief Services, 1997, *Annual Report 1996,* Baltimore, Maryland: CRS; CRS, 1998, *Annual Report 1997,* Baltimore, Maryland: CRS; CRS, 1999, *Annual Report 1998,* Baltimore, Maryland: CRS; and www.catholicrelief.org.

8. U.S. Catholic Mission Association (UCSMA), 1997, *U.S. Catholic Mission Handbook: Mission Inventory 1996-1997,* Washington, DC: U.S. Catholic Mission Association, 20-21. The information for Figure 5.1 and Table 5.6 also comes from this source.

9. Andrew D. Thompson, Ph.D., "What Really Happens to Our Former Volunteers: Leaders of Tomorrow's Society? Of the Church?," Washington, DC: Catholic Network of Volunteer Service, Lay Mission Handbook Series, Vol. 3 No. 5., n.d.; Angelyn Dries, 1998, *The Missionary Movement in American Catholic History,* Maryknoll, NY: Orbis Books.

6. PRIESTS

1. For example, CARA conducted a national random sample survey of pastors and recently ordained priests in 1998 that found that more than nine in ten priests and pastors cited those three items as important in their vocation decision. Other CARA studies of the presbyterate consistently bear out these findings.

2. CARA Catholic Poll, 2000.

3. Priests of the Eastern Churches are included in the numbers for both diocesan and religious priests in Figure 6.1, and thus are also included in total priests.

4. See, for example, Richard A. Schoenherr and Lawrence A. Young, 1993, *Full Pews and Empty Altars,* University of Wisconsin Press. Also see Lawrence A. Young, 1998, "Assessing and Updating the Schoenherr-Young Projections of Clergy Decline in the United States Roman Catholic Church," *Sociology of Religion,* 59: 7-23. CARA research is used for the 2000 distribution.

5. Based on CARA diocesan priest projection studies and other CARA demographic research on priests in the United States, the actual age distribution of all diocesan priests in 1999 is shown in Figure 6.3.

6. Priests of the Eastern Churches are not included in Figure 6.4, because eparchy territorial boundaries are often so broad that they cannot be assigned to just one region.

7. Compiled from individual diocesan figures as reported in *The Official Catholic Directory* for 1999.

8. The data in Figure 6.7 come from CARA's annual studies of seminary enrollments. These studies began in 1968, a year generally taken as the peak year for enrollments in Catholic seminaries. The data show increasingly larger differences between theologate enrollments of diocesan and religious priesthood candidates.

7. WOMEN AND MEN RELIGIOUS

1. Patricia Wittberg, SC, 1994, *The Rise and Decline of Catholic Religious Orders: A Social Movement Perspective*, Albany: State University of New York Press.

2. These definitions were clarified using P. Wittberg, SC, *The Rise and Decline of Catholic Religious Orders*, Chapter 3, "Contemporary Roman Catholic Religious Life: Some Preliminary Definitions."

3. Figures for religious priests, brothers, and sisters are from annual totals reported by dioceses to *The Official Catholic Directory* for each of those years.

4. Table 7.1 is from the *Annuario Pontificio*, the Vatican, for the years listed.

5. *Annuarium Statisticum Ecclesiae*. 1995. The Vatican.

6. Arthur Andersen, 1998, *Retirement Needs Survey – VII of United States Religious*. Report to the National Religious Retirement Office.

7. Figures for the current median age of religious women and men are from the National Religious Retirement Office of the USCCB, calculated for the 1998 calendar year. Figures for the current median age of religious priests are from current CARA research.

8. Figures on the numbers of religious engaged in teaching are from *The Official Catholic Directory*, 1999.

9. According to figures published by the U.S. Catholic Mission Association (UCSMA), 1997, *U.S. Catholic Mission Handbook: Mission Inventory 1996-1997*, Washington, DC: UCSMA.

10. These figures are based on the most recent estimates of religious in full-time active ministry only. Many other religious ministers in other areas, or in part-time or volunteer ministry, are not included in this table.

11. These data are drawn from Center for Applied Research in the Apostolate, 1999, *Emerging Religious Communities in the United States,* Washington, DC: CARA at Georgetown University. Also see Patricia Wittberg, SC and Mary E. Bendyna, RSM, 2000, "Portrait of Emerging Communities in the United States," *Horizon: Journal of the National Religious Vocation Conference*, 25, 2 (Winter 2000): 15-21.

8. DEACONS

1. These data on deacons and deacon candidates are from the USCCB Office of the Diaconate.

2. The demographic data on deacons are from the U.S. Bishops' Committee on the Permanent Diaconate, 1995, *A National Study on the Permanent Diaconate of the Catholic Church in the United States, 1994-1995* (Washington, D.C.: United States Catholic Conference).

9. LAY ECCLESIAL MINISTRY

1. From the final address of Anthony M. Pilla, Bishop of Cleveland, before the bishops as President of the Bishops' Conference in November 1998.

2. Table 9.1 on lay ecclesial ministers is calculated from estimates provided in Msgr. Phillip J. Murnion, 1992, *New Parish Ministers*, New York: National Pastoral Life Center, and Msgr. Phillip J. Murnion and David DeLambo, 1999, *Parishes and Parish Ministers*, New York: National Pastoral Life Center.

3. Geographical distribution of lay ecclesial ministers is from Msgr. Phillip J. Murnion, *New Parish Ministers*.

4. Msgr. Phillip J. Murnion and David DeLambo, *Parishes and Parish Ministers*.

5. Msgr. Phillip J. Murnion and David DeLambo, *Parishes and Parish Ministers*.

6. Pope Paul VI, *Gaudium et Spes* (*On the Church in the Modern World*, December 7, 1965). See Walter M. Abbot, SJ, ed., 1966, *The Documents of Vatican II*, New York: Guild Press/The America Press. The complete texts, along with a summary and links to related readings, can also be found at www.christusrex.org/www1/CDHN/v1.html.

Bibliography

Books and Articles

Abbot, Walter M., SJ, ed. 1966. *The Documents of Vatican II.* New York: Guild Press/The America Press.

Arthur Andersen. 1998. *Retirement Needs Survey - VII of United States Religious.* Report to the National Religious Retirement Office.

Association of Theological Schools. 1996. *Fact Book on Theological Education.* Pittsburgh: Association of Theological Schools.

Bagley, Ron, CJM, and John Roberto. 1996. *The Young Adult Research Report.*

Baumgaertner, Msgr. William L. and Francis Kelly Scheets, OSC. 1985. *Roman Catholic Seminaries and Theology Schools. NCEA Fact Book – National Summary of Key Issues: 1980-1984. Planning and Management Information.* Washington, DC: National Catholic Education Association, Seminary Department.

Bendyna, Mary E., RSM. 1999. *The Catholic Ethic in American Politics: Evidence from Survey Research.* Ph.D. Dissertation, Georgetown University.

Bishops' Committee on Vocations. 1996. *Future Full of Hope: A National Strategy for Vocations to the Priesthood and Religious Life in the Dioceses and Archdioceses of the United States.* January 1, 1996-December 31, 1998. Washington, DC: National Conference of Catholic Bishops.

Bradley, Martin B., et al. 1992. *Churches and Church Membership in the United States 1990: An Enumeration by Region, State and County Based on Data Reported for 133 Church Groupings.* Atlanta, GA: Glenmary Research Center.

Braun, Rev. Gary and Young Adult Panel. 1996. *If You Were in Our Shoes.* National Religious Vocations Conference. Video.

Brooks, Arlene E. 1980. *Profile of the Church-Related Volunteer.* Washington, DC: International Liaison, Inc.

Brown, Dorothy and Elizabeth McKeown. 1997. *The Poor Belong to Us: Catholic Charities and American Welfare.* Cambridge, MA and London: Harvard University Press.

Bryk, Anthony S., Valerie E. Lee, and Peter B. Holland. 1993. *Catholic Schools and the Common Good.* Cambridge, MA and London: Harvard University Press.

Burtchaell, James Tundstead, CSC. 1998. *The Dying of the Light: The Disengagement of Colleges and Universities from Their Christian Churches.* Grand Rapids, MI and Cambridge, U.K.: William B. Eerdmans Publishing Co.

Burns, J.A., CSC. 1912. *The Growth and Development of the Catholic School System in the United States.* New York: Benziger Brothers.

Burnson, Matthew, ed. 1999. *Our Sunday Visitor's Catholic Almanac 2000.* Huntington, IN: Our Sunday Visitor, Inc.

Butler, Francis J., ed. 1994. *American Catholic Identity: Essays in an Age of Change.* Kansas City, MO: Sheed and Ward.

213

Byers, David, ed. 1985. *The Parish in Transition: Proceedings of a Conference on the American Catholic Parish.* Washington, DC: Foundations and Donors Interested in Catholic Activities.

Cadena, Gilbert. 1998. "Latinos and Latinas in the Catholic Church: Cohesion and Conflict." In Madeleine Cousineau, *Religion in a Changing World: Comparative Studies in Theology.* Westport, CT and London: Praeger. 109-118.

Carter, Martin J. 1988. "The Catholic Priesthood: An African American Perspective." In *One Faith, One Lord, One Baptism: The Hopes and Experiences of the Black Community in the Archdiocese of New York.* New York: Archdiocese of New York.

Center for Applied Research in the Apostolate. 1968. *The CARA-Serra Vocations Conference.* Washington, DC.

Center for Applied Research in the Apostolate. 1988. *CARA Symposium on Vocations to the Roman Catholic Priesthood.* Washington, DC.

Center for Applied Research in the Apostolate. 1999. *Emerging Religious Communities in the United States.* Washington, DC.

Center for Marriage and Family. 1995. *Marriage Preparation in the Catholic Church: Getting It Right.* Omaha, NE: Center for Marriage and Family, Creighton University.

Cisco, Bede Donald. 1986. *Changes in Catholic Undergraduate Seminary Education, 1960-1985: A Population Ecology Perspective.* Ed.D. Dissertation, Teachers' College, Columbia University.

Coriden, James A., Thomas J. Green, and Donald E. Heintschel. 1985. *The Code of Canon Law: A Text and Commentary.* New York: Paulist Press / The Canon Law Society of America.

Cousineau, Madeleine. 1998. *Religion in a Changing World: Comparative Studies in Theology.* Westport, CT and London: Praeger.

Cozzens, Donald B. 2000. *The Changing Face of the Priesthood.* Collegeville, MN: Liturgical Press.

Crews, Clyde F. 1994. *American and Catholic: A Popular History of Catholicism in the United States.* Cincinnati, OH: St. Anthony Messenger Press.

Cunniggim, Merrimon. 1994. *Uneasy Partners: The College and the Church.* Nashville: Abingdon Press.

Curran, Robert Emmett, SJ. 1993. *The Bicentennial History of Georgetown University*, Vol. I, *From Academy to University.* Washington, DC: Georgetown University Press.

Cuyler, Cornelius M., SS. 1969. *The Changing Direction of the Seminary Today.* Washington, DC: Center for Applied Research in the Apostolate.

D'Antonio, William V., James D. Davidson, Dean R. Hoge, and Ruth A. Wallace. 1989. *American Catholic Laity in a Changing Church.* Kansas City, MO: Sheed and Ward.

D'Antonio, William V., James D. Davidson, Dean R. Hoge, and Ruth A. Wallace. 1996. *Laity, American and Catholic: Transforming the Church.* Kansas City, MO: Sheed and Ward.

D'Arcy, Paul F. and Eugene C. Kennedy. 1965. *The Genius of the Apostolate: Personal Growth in the Candidate, the Seminarian, and the Priest.* New York: Sheed and Ward.

Davidson, James D., et al. 1997. *The Search for Common Ground: What Unites and Divides Catholic Americans.* Huntington, IN: Our Sunday Visitor, Inc.

Davis, Cyprian, OSB. 1990. *The History of Black Catholics in the United States.* New York: Crossroad.

DeRego, Frank R., Jr., and James D. Davidson. 1998. "Catholic Deacons: A Lesson in Role Conflict and Ambiguity." In Madeleine Cousineau, *Religion in a Changing World: Comparative Studies in Theology.* Westport, CT and London: Praeger. 89-98.

Díaz-Stevens, Ana Maria and Anthony M. Stevens-Arroyo. 1998. *Recognizing the Latino Religious Resurgence in U.S. Religion: The Emmaus Paradigm.* U.S.A.: Westview Press.

Dolan, Jay P., SJ. 1978. *Catholic Revivalism: The American Experience, 1830-1900.* Notre Dame, IN: University of Notre Dame Press.

Dolan, Jay P., SJ. 1992. *The American Catholic Experience: A History from Colonial Times to the Present.* Notre Dame, IN: University of Notre Dame Press.

Dolan, Jay P., R. Scott Appleby, Patricia Byme and Debra Campbell. 1989. *Transforming Parish Ministry: The Changing Roles of Catholic Clergy, Laity, and Women Religious.* New York: Crossroad.

Dries, Angelyn, OSF. 1998. *The Missionary Movement in American Catholic History.* Maryknoll, NY: Orbis Books.

Ebaugh, Helen R. 1988. *Becoming an Ex: The Process of Role Exit.* Chicago: University of Chicago Press.

Egan, Eileen. 1988. *Catholic Relief Services: The Beginning Years: For the Life of the World.* New York: Catholic Relief Services.

Evans, Placidus. 1951. *An Investigation into the Origins of Vocations to the Teaching Brotherhoods.* Washington, DC: The Catholic University.

Faris, John D. 1992. *The Eastern Catholic Churches: Constitution and Governance According to the Code of Canons of the Eastern Churches.* New York: Saint Maron Publications.

Fee, Joan L., Andrew M. Greeley, William C. McCready, and Teresa A. Sullivan. 1981. *Young Catholics: A Report to the Knights of Columbus.* New York: Sadlier.

Felknor, Laurie, ed. 1989. *The Crisis in Religious Vocations: An Inside View.* New York: Paulist Press.

Fichter, Joseph H., SJ. 1961. *Religion as an Occupation: A Study in the Sociology of Professions.* Notre Dame, IN: University of Notre Dame Press.

Fichter, Joseph H., SJ. 1968. *America's Forgotten Priests – What They Are Saying.* Cambridge, MA: Harvard University Press.

Fichter, Joseph H., SJ. 1993. *The Sociology of Good Works: Research in Catholic America.* Chicago: Loyola University Press.

Finke, Roger and Rodney Stark. 1992. *The Churching of America, 1776-1990: Winners and Losers in Our Religious Economy.* New Brunswick, NJ: Rutgers University Press.

Finn, Daniel, Zeni Fox, John O'Malley, and Robert Schwartz. 1989. *Theology of Priesthood and Seminary Formation: Issues of Assembly II.* Washington, DC: National Catholic Educational Association.

Fogarty, J.C. 1988. *The Catholic Priest: His Identity and Values: A Ministerial Profile of the Joliet Presbyterate.* Kansas City, MO: Sheed and Ward.

Foundations and Donors Interested in Catholic Activities. 1988. *U.S. Catholic Seminaries and Their Future.* Washington, DC: U.S. Catholic Conference.

Foundations and Donors Interested in Catholic Activities. 1991. *Exception and Promise: A Look at Catholic Vocations. Proceedings of a Symposium.* Washington, DC: Foundations and Donors Interested in Catholic Activities.

Froehle, Bryan T. 1996. *New Directions in Youth Ministry: A National Study of Catholic Youth Ministry Program Participants.* Washington, DC: Center for Applied Research in the Apostolate.

Froehle, Bryan T. 1997. *Survey of Catholic Youth and Parents Connected with Parish Programs: Findings and Implications for Vocations.* Washington, DC: Center for Applied Research in the Apostolate.

Froehle, Bryan T., ed. 1997. *CARA Compendium of Vocations Research.* Washington, DC: Center for Applied Research in the Apostolate.

Froehle, Bryan T. 1998. *Diocesan and Eparchial Pastoral Councils: A National Profile.* Washington, DC: Center for Applied Research in the Apostolate.

Froehle, Bryan T. and Mary E. Bendyna, RSM. 1999. *Diocesan Profile of Catechetical Ministry: An NCCL, NCEA and USCC Joint Project.* Washington, DC: Center for Applied Research in the Apostolate.

Gallup, George, Jr. 1989. *The People's Religion: American Faith in the 90s.* New York: Macmillan Publishing Co.

Gallup, George. 1991. *Emerging Trends.* 13, no. 7 (Sept.).

Gallup, George, Jr. and Jim Castelli. 1987. *The American Catholic People: Their Beliefs, Practices, and Values.* Garden City, NY: Doubleday and Co., Inc.

Garland, Sr. Mary. 1951. *Certain Domestic Factors in the Choice of a Religious Vocation.* Washington, DC: The Catholic University.

Gaustad, Edwin Scott. 1962. *Historical Atlas of Religion in America.* New York and Evanston: Harper and Row Publishers.

Gautier, Mary L. and Bryan T. Froehle. 1999. *National Parish Inventory: Project Report.* Washington, DC: Center for Applied Research in the Apostolate.

Gavin, Donald P. 1962. *The National Conference of Catholic Charities, 1910-1960.* Milwaukee: Catholic Life Publications/Bruce Press.

Gillespie, Francis, SJ, and Eleace King, IHM. 1989. *Attitudes of Minority Students Toward Jesuits, Religious Life, and the Ordained Priesthood.* Washington, DC: Center for Applied Research in the Apostolate.

Gillis, Chester. 1999. *Roman Catholicism in America.* New York: Columbia University Press.

Glenn, Norval and Ruth Hyland. 1991. "Religious Identity and the Conventional Wisdom." *Catholics/U.S.A.* 51.

Gottemoeller, Doris, RSM. 1996. "Inheritors of the Promise, Midwives of the Future." *Horizon: Journal of the National Religious Vocation Conference.* Convocation 1996 Issue.

Greeley, Andrew M. 1972. *The Catholic Priest in the United States: Sociological Investigations.* Washington, DC: United States Catholic Conference.

Greeley, Andrew M. 1972. *The Denominational Society: A Sociological Approach to Religion in America.* Glenview, IL: Scott, Foresman and Co.

Greeley, Andrew M. 1972. *Priests in the United States: Reflections on a Survey.* Garden City, NY: Doubleday.

Greeley, Andrew M. 1981. *The Religious Imagination.* New York: William H. Sadlier.

Greeley, Andrew M. 1985. *American Catholics Since the Council: An Unauthorized Report.* Chicago: Thomas More Press.

Greeley, Andrew M. 1989. *Religious Change in America.* Cambridge, MA and London: Harvard University Press.

Greeley, Andrew M. 1990. *The Catholic Myth: The Behavior and Beliefs of American Catholics.* New York: Collier Books.

Greeley, Andrew M. 1991. "The Demography of American Catholics." In Helen R. Ebaugh, ed., *Vatican II and American Catholicism.* Greenwich, CT: JAI Press. 37-56.

Greeley, Andrew M. 1995. *Religion as Poetry.* New Brunswick, NJ: Transaction Publications.

Hagan, Bishop John R. 1945. "Some Factors in the Development of Religious Vocations of Women." *Journal of Religious Instruction.* XV, 7: 621-628, 8: 712-718, 9: 794-800.

Hayes, Diana L. and Cyprian Davis, OSB, eds. 1998. *Taking Down Our Harps: Black Catholics in the United States.* Maryknoll, NY: Orbis Books.

Hemrick, Eugene and Dean R. Hoge. 1985. *Seminarians in Theology: A National Profile.* Sponsored by Bishops' Committee on Priestly Formation, NCCB, NCEA, Assembly of Ordinaries and Rectors/Presidents of Theologates. Conducted by Office of Research, USCC-NCCB in conjunction with the Center for the Study of Youth Development of the Catholic University of America.

Hemrick, Eugene and Dean R. Hoge. 1987. *Seminary Life and Visions of the Priesthood: A National Survey of Seminarians.* Washington, DC: National Catholic Educational Association, Seminary Department.

Hemrick, Eugene and Dean R. Hoge. 1991. *A Survey of Priests Ordained Five to Nine Years.* Washington, DC: National Catholic Educational Association, Seminary Department.

Hemrick, Eugene and Robert Wister. 1993. *Readiness for Theological Studies: A Study of Faculty Perceptions on the Readiness of Seminarians.* Washington, DC: National Catholic Educational Association, Seminary Department.

Hemrick, Eugene F. and James J. Walsh. 1993. *Seminarians in the Nineties: A National Study of Seminarians in Theology.* Washington, DC: National Catholic Educational Association, Seminary Department.

Hoge, Dean R. 1985. *The Future of Catholic Leadership: Responses to the Priest Shortage.* Kansas City, MO: Sheed and Ward.

Hoge, Dean R. 1999. "What is Most Central to Being a Catholic?" *National Catholic Reporter.* 36, no. 2 (Oct. 29, 1999).

Hoge, Dean R. and Boguslaw Augustyn. 1997. "Financial Contributions to Catholic Parishes: A Nationwide Study of Determinants." *Review of Religious Research.* 39, 1 (Sept.): 46-60.

O'Grady, John. 1971 (1931). *Catholic Charities in the United States: History and Problems.* New York: Arno Press (Washington, DC: National Conference of Catholic Charities).

O'Hara, Joseph and Thomas P. Ferguson. 1993. "Seminary Enrollment Statistics: A Review of the Past Quarter Century (1966-1991)." *The New CARA Seminary Forum.* 1, no. 2: 9-20.

One Faith, One Lord, One Baptism: The Hopes and Experiences of the Black Community in the Archdiocese of New York. 1988. New York: Archdiocese of New York.

Phelps, Jamie T., OP, ed. 1997. *Black and Catholic: The Challenge and Gift of Black Folk: Contributions of African American Experience and Thought to Catholic Theology.* Milwaukee: Marquette University Press.

Potvin, Raymond H. 1985. *Seminarians of the Eighties: A National Survey.* Washington, DC: National Catholic Educational Association, Seminary Department.

Potvin, Raymond H. and Felipe L. Muncada. 1989. *Seminary Outcomes: Perseverance and Withdrawal.* Washington, DC: The Catholic University Institute of Social and Behavioral Research.

Potvin, Raymond H. and Antanas Suziedelis. 1969. *Seminarians of the Sixties: A National Survey.* Washington, DC: Center for Applied Research in the Apostolate.

Putz, Louis J., CSC. 1956. *The Catholic Church, U.S.A.* Chicago: Fides Publishers.

Raymond, John, M.A. 2000. *Catholics on the Internet, 2000-2001.* Roseville, CA: Prima Publishing.

Reese, Thomas J., SJ. 1992. *A Flock of Shepherds: The National Conference of Catholic Bishops.* Kansas City, MO: Sheed and Ward.

Riebe-Estrella, Gary, SVD. 1996. "American Catholic Cultural Shifts and Religious Life." *Horizon: Journal of the National Religious Vocation Conference.* Convocation 1996 Issue.

Roccasalvo, Joan L. 1992. *The Eastern Catholic Churches: An Introduction to Their Worship and Spirituality.* Collegeville, MN: Liturgical Press.

Ryan, Mary Perkins. 1964. *Are Parochial Schools the Answer?* New York: Holt, Reinhart and Winston.

Ryle, Msgr. Edward J., 1997. "Catholic Charities, Catholic Identity, and the Mission of the Church: Some Approaches for Catholic Charities." In Jo-Ann Leitch, ed. *Who Do You Say We Are? Perspectives on Catholic Identity in Catholic Charities.* Alexandria, VA: Catholic Charities USA.

Sarther, Catherine and William McCready. 1983. *Vocational Decisions: A Comparison Between Women Who Decided to Enter and Those Who Decided Not to Enter a Canonical Religious Community.* Chicago: National Sisters Vocation Conference.

Scheets, Francis Kelly, OSC. 1979. *CARA/Lilly Study Handbook for National Task Force Members.* Washington, DC: Center for Applied Research in the Apostolate.

Schoenherr, Richard A. and Annemette Sorensen. 1981. *From the Second Vatican Council to the Second Millennium: Decline and Change in the U.S. Catholic*

Church. Madison: University of Wisconsin Comparative Religious Organization Studies, Respondent Report 5.

Schoenherr, Richard A. and Annemette Sorensen. 1982. "Social Change in Religious Organizations: Consequences of Clergy Decline in the U.S. Catholic Church." *Sociological Analysis.* 43: 23-52.

Schoenherr, Richard A. and Lawrence A. Young. 1988. "Organizational Demography and Structural Change in the Roman Catholic Church." Paper presented at the CARA Symposium on Vocations to the Roman Catholic Priesthood, March 1988.

Schoenherr, Richard A and Lawrence A. Young. 1990. *The Catholic Priest in the United States: Demographic Investigations.* Vol. 3, "Final Report: National, Regional, and Local Trends and Projections of Incardinated Diocesan Priest Population, 1996-2005." Report prepared for the United States Catholic Conference.

Schoenherr, Richard A and Lawrence A. Young. 1993. *Full Pews and Empty Altars.* Madison, WI: University of Wisconsin Press.

Schuth, Katarina, OSF. 1989. *Reason for the Hope: The Futures of Roman Catholic Theologates.* Wilmington, DE: Michael Glazier.

Schuth, Katarina, OSF. 1993. "Seminarians Today as Church Leaders Tomorrow." In *Seminarians in the Nineties: A National Study of Seminarians in Theology.* Washington, DC: National Catholic Education Association.

Schuth, Katarina, OSF. 1999. *Seminaries, Theologates and the Future of Church Ministry: An Analysis of Trends and Transitions.* Collegeville, MN: Liturgical Press.

Schweickert, Jeanne, SSSF. 1987. *Who's Entering Religious Life? An NCRVD National Study.* Chicago: National Conference of Religious Vocation Directors.

Shaughnessy, Gerald. 1969 (1925). *Has the Immigrant Kept the Faith? A Study of Immigration and Catholic Growth in the United States, 1790 to 1920.* New York: Arno Press.

Shields, Joseph J. and Mary Jeanne Verdieck. 1985. *Religious Life in the United States: The Experience of Men's Communities.* Washington, DC: Center for Applied Research in the Apostolate.

Stewart, George C., Jr. 1994. *Marvels of Charity: History of American Sisters and Nuns.* Huntington, IN: Our Sunday Visitor, Inc.

Thompson, Andrew D. n.d. "What Really Happens to Our Former Volunteers: Leaders of Tomorrow's Society? Of the Church?" Lay Mission Handbook Series. Vol. 3, no. 5. Washington, DC: Catholic Network of Volunteer Service.

Tropman, John E. 1995. *The Catholic Ethic in American Society: An Exploration of Values.* San Francisco: Jossey-Bass Publishers.

U.S. Catholic Mission Association. 1997. *U.S. Catholic Mission Handbook: Mission Inventory 1996-1997.* Washington, DC: UCSMA.

U.S. Census Bureau. *Statistical Abstract of the United States: 1998.* Washington, DC: U.S. Department of Commerce, Economics and Statistics Administration, Bureau of the Census. This can also be downloaded as a PDF file from the U.S. Census Bureau website at www.census.gov.

United States Department of Commerce, Bureau of the Census. 1929-1930. *Religious Bodies: 1926.* 2 vols. U.S.A.: Government Printing Office.

Verdieck, Mary Jeanne, Joseph J. Shields and Dean R. Hoge. 1988. "Role Commitment Processes Revisited: American Catholic Priests 1970 and 1985." *Journal for the Scientific Study of Religion* 27: 524-535.

Wallace, Ruth A. 1992. *They Call Her Pastor: A New Role for Catholic Women.* Albany, NY: State University of New York Press.

Walsh, James, John Mayer, James Castelli, Eugene Hemrick, Melvin Blanchette, and Paul Theroux. 1995. *Grace Under Pressure: What Gives Life to American Priests: A Study of Effective Priests Ordained Ten to Thirty Years.* Washington, DC: National Catholic Education Association, Seminary Department.

Wittberg, Patricia, SC. 1994. *The Rise and Decline of Catholic Religious Orders: A Social Movement Perspective.* Albany: State University of New York Press.

Wittberg, Patricia, SC. 1996. *Pathways to Re-Creating Religious Communities.* New York: Paulist Press.

Wittberg, Patricia, SC and Mary E. Bendyna, RSM. 2000. "Portrait of Emerging Communities in the United States." *Horizon: Journal of the National Religious Vocation Conference.* 25, no. 2 (Winter 2000): 15-21.

Young, Lawrence A. 1998. "Assessing and Updating the Schoenherr-Young Projections of Clergy Decline in the United States Roman Catholic Church." *Sociology of Religion.* 59, no. 1 (Spring 1998): 7-23.

Young, Lawrence A. and Richard A. Schoenherr. 1992. "The Changing Age Distribution and Theological Attitudes of Catholic Priests Revisited." *Sociological Analysis* 53: 73-87.

Yuhaus, Cassian J., CP. 1984. *Vocations to the Priesthood and Religious Life in the Church Today: A Seminar.* Washington, DC: Center for Applied Research in the Apostolate.

Websites

The principal guide to sources on Catholicism available online is John Raymond, M.A., *Catholics on the Internet, 2000-2001.* Below is a basic list of websites that proved useful for this study and that can serve for initial explorations.

Adherents.com-Religious Statistics
www.adherents.com/adhloc/index_adherentsWhere.html
Statistical information for all religious bodies.

American Religious Data Archive
www.thearda.com.
Excellent source of data sets on religious bodies.

American University–Catholic Files
http://listserv.american.edu/catholic/
Numerous transcriptions of papal encyclicals, Church teachings, and documents pertaining to religious institutes; links to other Catholic websites.

Catholic Campus Ministry of America
www.udayton.edu/~ccma/
National office of the CCMA is in Dayton; links to local CCM websites and the
mail list of the National Catholic Student Coalition.

.Catholic Charities USA
www.catholiccharitiesusa.org

Catholic Religious Institutes and Organizations
www.iol.ie/~readout/inst.html
A work-in-progress list of religious institutes' web pages.

Catholic Health Association
www.chausa.org

Catholic Information Center on the Internet™ (CICI)
www.catholic.net
Multiple links, including Catholic World News, the Holy See, Dioceses and Mass
Times online, teachings, doctrines, magisterium and Church documentation,
websites of religious institutes, and international Catholic sites.

Catholic Information Network
www.cin.org
Particularly helpful search engine.

Catholic Online Internet Services
www.catholic.org/index2.html

Catholic Relief Services
www.catholicrelief.org
The website of the CRS, with information on the organization's history, current
projects, employment and volunteer opportunities, and links to international
organizations.

1983 Code of Canon Law
www.prairienet.org/nrpcatholic/cicmenu.html
Available in English, French, Spanish and Latin; site includes search engine.

Documents from the Second Vatican Council
www.christusrex.org/www1/CDHN/v1.html
This site also contains a summary and useful links for related information
pertaining to the Council.

Eternal Word Television Network–Document Library
www.ewtn.com
Document library; site includes search engine; papal and episcopal decrees
available, as well as relevant periodical citations.

George Gallup Jr.'s Princeton Religious Research Center
www.prrc.com
Latest Gallup Poll statistics; information available for the past 60 years.

New Advent
www.newadvent.org
Links to the Catholic Encyclopedia Project, online versions of the *Summa Theologica*, writings of the Early Church Fathers, the Bible and Concordances, the Holy See, AlaPadre, and much more.

United States Bureau of the Census
www.census.gov
For the *Statistical Abstracts of the United States 1998* (most recent year available), as well as other sources of information pertaining to the U.S. population.

The Vatican
www.vatican.va

Index

abortion, 32
academic freedom, 84
acolytes, 108
ACORN (Association of Communities Organized for Reform Now), 99
Africa, 12 (table 1.7), 104 (table 5.11)
African Americans: characteristics of parishes with significant numbers of, 58; contrast of Protestant and Catholic attitudes toward government action regarding, 34 (table 2.9); deacons who are, 144; in formation programs for lay ecclesial ministers, 164, 165 (fig. 9.5); lay ecclesial ministers who are, 155; Mass attendance by, 23 (table 2.1); men and women religious who are, 135; in metropolitan and non-metropolitan areas, 53; number of Catholics who are, 16-17; overview of demographics for, 6-8; in specific states, 18
Aid to Dependent Children, 96
Alexian Brothers, 89
Apostolicam Actuositatem (Vatican II, Decree on the Laity), 164
archdioceses, 46-47
Armenian Church, 40, 42, 43 (table 3.4), 146
Asia, 11-12, 104 (table 5.11). *See also* Asians
Asians: characteristics of parishes with significant numbers of, 58; deacons who are, 144; in formation programs for lay ecclesial ministers, 164, 165 (fig. 9.5); Mass attendance by, 23 (table 2.1); men and women religious who are, 135; in metropolitan and non-metropolitan areas, 53; number of Catholics who are, 16-17; in specific states, 18

Baby Boomers, 4. *See also* Vatican II
baptisms: method of computing, 208n.3; in metropolitan and non-metropolitan areas, 27 (table 2.2), 53 (table 3.16); parish size and, 55; ratios to other sacraments, 26-27, 207n.13; statistics on, for parishes with specific racial/ethnic identities, 58 (table 3.19); statistics on infant, 13 (table 1.8)
Big Brother organization, 95
Big Sister organization, 95
birth rates of immigrants, 10
bishops, 152-53. *See also* United States Conference of Catholic Bishops
brothers. *See* men religious

Canon Law, 46, 206n.6
Caribbean, the, 104 (table 5.11)
Caritas Internationalis, 98
Carroll, Charles, 14
Carroll, Daniel, 14
Carroll, John, 14, 126
catechesis, 26
catechists, 108
Catholic Campaign for Human Development, 88, 98-99, 105
Catholic Charities USA, 96-97. *See also* National Conference of Catholic Charities
Catholic Daughters of America, 95, 153
"Catholic ethic," the, 34
Catholic Health Association of the United States, 90, 91
Catholic Healthcare Association, 105
Catholic imagination, the, 33-35
Catholic Relief Services, 88, 96, 100-105
Catholic University of America, the, 82, 84, 95, 96
Cavanaugh, John J., 82-83

225

58; deacons who are, 144, 148; distribution of parishes involved in ministry to, 56 (map 3.2); in formation programs for lay ecclesial ministers, 164, 165 (fig. 9.5); lay ecclesial ministers who are, 155; Mass attendance by, 23-24; men and women religious who are, 135; in metropolitan and non-metropolitan areas, 53; number of Catholics among, 16-18; overview of twentieth-century presence of, in the United States, 6; in specific states, 18

Hoey, Jane, 95-96

Holy Cross College, 83

hospitals, 88, 89-91, 92 (map 5.1)

housing, 96

identity: Catholic, of recent immigrants, 12; elements of Catholic, 27-28; universities and Catholic, 83-85

immigrants: altering religious affiliation by, 204n.13; distribution of, 6-8; impact of, on Catholic population growth, 10-12; number of, in 1970 and 1993, 204n.11; settlement patterns of, 207n.8; sources of data on, 204n.9; statistics for, since 1991, 12 (table 1.7); statistics on European, 11 (table 1.6)

income, household, 16 (table 1.11)

institutions, 37-38. *See also specific institutions and types of institutions*

intermarriage: Catholic population increases and, 13; distribution of, 25 (map 2.1); in metropolitan and non-metropolitan areas, 27 (table 2.2); overall statistics on, 24 (fig. 2.1)

International Cooperation for Development and Solidarity, 98

Ireland, Bishop John, 65

Jesuits, 66, 73, 83

John XXIII, Pope, 68

Kennedy, John F., 29

Knights of Columbus, 153

Ladies of Charity, 89, 93, 95

laity: the Catholic Campaign for Human Development and, 99 (table 5.7); Catholic Relief Services and, 101 (table 5.8); foreign missions and, 103-5; social services and, 95, 106. *See also* lay ecclesial ministers; lay ministry

Lange, Mother Mary Elizabeth, 8

Latin America, 11-12, 104 (table 5.11)

Latinos. *See* Hispanics/Latinos

lay ecclesial ministers: and administration of parishes without resident pastors, 61; age of participants in formation programs for, 163-64; ages of, 154-55; conclusions regarding, 164-66; diocesan support for, 158-59; educational background of those in formation programs for, 159; emerging role for, 157-58; geographic distribution of, 156 (map 9.1), 157; geographic distribution of formation programs for, 161 (map 9.2); in metropolitan and non-metropolitan areas, 53 (table 3.16); number of, 153 (table 9.1); number of persons enrolled in formation programs for, 160; overview of, 151-53; parish size and, 55; and parish staffs in various regions, 61 (table 3.22); profile of formation programs for, 162-63; racial and ethnic backgrounds of, 155; racial and ethnic backgrounds of persons in formation programs for, 164; statistics on, for parishes with specific racial/ethnic identities, 58 (table 3.19); twentieth-century trends regarding, 153-54. *See also* laity; lay ministry

lay ministry, 107-8. *See also* lay ecclesial ministers

leadership, 21-22

lectors, 108, 151

Leo XIII, Pope, 94

liberalism, 31-33

Lower Plains region. *See* regions of the United States Conference of Catholic Bishops

205ff

p68 schools?
74 teachers
Procorate 146